Dignity, Justice, and the Nazi Data Debate

Dignity, Justice, and the Nazi Data Debate

On Violating the Violated Anew

Carol V. A. Quinn

LEXINGTON BOOKS
Lanham • Boulder • New York • London

Published by Lexington Books
An imprint of The Rowman & Littlefield Publishing Group, Inc.
4501 Forbes Boulevard, Suite 200, Lanham, Maryland 20706
www.rowman.com

Unit A, Whitacre Mews, 26-34 Stannary Street, London SE11 4AB

Copyright © 2018 by The Rowman & Littlefield Publishing Group, Inc.

Chapter 4 (Poetry by Nelly Sachs): "Chorus of the Rescued" translated by Michael Roloff from O THE CHIMNEYS by Nelly Sachs. Translation copyright © 1967, renewed 1995 by Farrar, Straus & Giroux, Inc. Reprinted by permission of Farrar, Straus and Giroux.

Chapter 4 (Poetry by Leivick): Used with permission from University of Illinois Press.

Chapter 4 (Poetry by Feldman): "To the Six Million" from COLLECTED POEMS, 1954-2004 by Irving Feldman, copyright © 2004 by Irving Feldman. Used by permission of Schocken Books, an imprint of the Knopf Doubleday Publishing Group, a division of Penguin Random House LLC. All rights reserved.

All rights reserved. No part of this book may be reproduced in any form or by any electronic or mechanical means, including information storage and retrieval systems, without written permission from the publisher, except by a reviewer who may quote passages in a review.

British Library Cataloguing in Publication Information Available

The hardback edition of this book was previously catalogued by the Library of Congress as follows:

Library of Congress Cataloging-in-Publication Data

Names: Quinn, Carol Viola Anne, author.
Title: Dignity, justice, and the Nazi data debate : on violating the violated anew / Carol V.A. Quinn.
Description: Lanham : Lexington Books, [2018] | Includes bibliographical references and index.
Identifiers: LCCN 2017055817 (print) | LCCN 2017057669 (ebook) |
  ISBN 9781498550031 (electronic) | ISBN 9781498550024 (cloth : alk. paper) |
  ISBN 9781498550048 (pbk. : alk. paper)
Subjects: LCSH: Human experimentation in medicine—Moral and ethical aspects. |
  Medicine—Research—Moral and ethical aspects. | Medical ethics.
Classification: LCC R853.H8 (ebook) | LCC R853.H8 Q56 2018 (print) |
  DDC 174.2/8—dc23
LC record available at https://lccn.loc.gov/2017055817

For Samuel Gorovitz
In Loving Memory of Robert Lawrence Quinn

*An example of epistemic
Injustice.
And what it would mean
To take seriously
The survivors'
Claims.*

Contents

Preface		xi
Acknowledgments		xv
Introduction		1
1	An Overview of the Debate	11
2	Kant's Conception of Dignity and How It Fails to Capture Survivors' Claims of Harm	27
3	On Finding an Adequate Conception of Dignity	47
4	Trauma, the Self, and Controlling the Nazi Data	67
5	Nazi Data: Transparent, Evil, and Transparently Evil	89
6	Epistemic Injustice and the Survivors' Claims to Moral Expertise	115
Bibliography		133
Index		143
About the Author		147

Preface

When I started my undergraduate degree, I wanted to be a veterinarian. Having been the neighborhood "veterinarian" for the injured and stray since my early teens, I thought that this was my calling. But after working at veterinary clinics and teaching hospitals, I quickly discovered that I could not stomach seeing animals' insides without passing out. So I abandoned that idea and wanted to save animals in a different way—as an animal ethicist.

My grandfather wouldn't have any of it. While he thought that this was a noble calling, he pressed upon me the importance of *human* ethics, and in particular, humans and unethical experimentation. My grandfather was a Jew and he would often tell me about the Holocaust and the unethical experiments carried out by the Nazis in the concentration camps. His mother (my great grandmother) was a Russian-Ukrainian Jew (Ukraine then was under the Russian Empire), and he would always impress upon me that it was a matter of luck that his mother and her family did not end up in the camps. His mother's family came to Long Island in the early 1900s, just escaping a pogrom. Were it not for their move to Long Island, his mother might have died in one of those camps.

My grandfather had undergraduate degrees in philosophy and English. He had been accepted into graduate school and was going to study under philosopher Bertrand Russell when his father died in his arms and his plans changed. He would care for his mother. My grandfather would spend hours talking to me about the Holocaust and the experiments in the camps. He sparked a real passion in me for this project.

While I was in graduate school, I came across medical ethicist Arthur Caplan's 1992 edited collection, *When Medicine Went Mad: Bioethics and the Holocaust*, with essays from participants in the first ever (and only) international conference on the ethics of using Nazi medical data. I wrote to Caplan and asked him whether he had additional materials that he could share. I was thrilled when he sent me a big packet of newspaper clippings and other writings detailing the conference, including testimony from some of the conference participants. Much of the testimony that I present in this work comes from that packet of materials.

As I read through the materials, and especially the way that the conference played out, it became clear that there was something deeply unjust about the way that survivors were being treated. Their claims were dismissed as so much nonsense coming from emotional cripples tied to the past. It also became clear that the survivors had something important to say—the same arguments kept coming up. They argued that by using the data (without their consent) we continued to harm them, to harm their dignity. They argued that they are the "living data" of the experiments. They argued that they are the ones who should control the data (who should decide what should be done with it). They argued that they alone are the *real* experts in the debate—not the researchers and medical ethicists, despite their "credentials." They argued that the Nazi data is evil (*really* evil, not merely symbolically evil), and we become morally tainted by using it. The survivors had something important to say, and nobody seemed to be paying attention.

I decided that I needed to make sense of the survivors' claims, to be their advocate, to make the strongest case. At about this time I met the late Claudia Card, who would become one of my favorite mentors. She was working on a project on evil—what would become her book *The Atrocity Paradigm*. We traveled to DC together to research at the US Holocaust Memorial Museum. We would walk around DC, taking in the sites, talking about evil and dignity. These talks were invaluable to me. Soon thereafter, I would be going to Japan to give a lecture on taking survivors of Nazi medical experiments seriously at the World Congress of the International Network on Feminist Approaches to Bioethics (in conjunction with the International Association of Bioethics). I had come up with a social conception of dignity that I believed made sense of some of the survivors' claims.

I left my talk crying. Audience members challenged me: Why should I take such irrational people seriously? What was my sample size? As a philosopher, I didn't really know about sample sizes. What was I doing? Was I in over my head? I almost gave up on my project, when I was approached by an Israeli bioethicist who invited me to Israel to research at Yad Vashem under then-director Yehuda Bauer, to talk with survivors and their children, give lectures, and meet with members of the Knesset. What an opportunity! I talked with psychologists of trauma about how to be a sensitive listener. I met with a professor of Hebrew to start learning the language. A travel grant got me to Israel. I stayed most of the time with an Israeli family. The husband, Shlomo, was a retired professor at Hebrew University. Talking with survivors and their children, and with Yosef Lapid, a member of the Knesset, I was encouraged to continue my project. They all echoed the claims made by the survivors that I had come across in my reading. I *was* onto something, and something important.

As I worked on my project, I felt that it was inadequate. I couldn't pull it all together. Looking back now, I realized that I didn't have all of the conceptual tools to really make sense of their claims. I published a few articles on the topic over the years, but something was missing. I learned about epistemic arrogance (before José Medina popularized the term) in chats with Linda Martín Alcoff. But it would be years before Miranda Fricker would write her insightful book on epistemic injustice. I learned about the connection between emotions and knowledge in chats with Michael Stocker, but it would be years before there would really be a lot of work done on emotional insight. Further, few at the time were engaging in research on testimony and moral expertise.

It finally really came together when I read Maurice Merleau-Ponty's *Phenomenology of Perception* and especially his conception of the self and its relationship to cultural objects. Now I was able to make sense of two of the survivors' more controversial claims: that they are the "living data," and the data is evil and we become morally tainted when we use it. Then in January 2014, while reading the *New York Times*, I came upon Chuck Klosterman's piece in *The Ethicist* entitled "Can Data Be Evil?" in which he argues that the Nazi data is essentially neutral, and so we should use it to save lives. He admits that his conclusion is "cold heartedly clinical," but claims that this is different from being unethical.

Fifty people commented on his essay. They all gave familiar arguments for and against using the Nazi data, but noticeably absent was any seeming concern for the survivors and what *they* want. Attitudes hadn't changed since the 1989 conference. It struck me then that it was time to revisit my project, all the more so that the survivors are very old and won't be with us much longer. Even so, one of the survivors' insights is that it doesn't matter whether they are all gone. So long as we continue to use the data, we continue to harm our community and ourselves—neither the victims nor the evil ever "leave" the data. Further, this case is emblematic of other historical disputes concerning whether to use data gained unethically, disputes that include victims' (silent) voices.

There are limitations to my project, including the methodological problem of speaking for others. But I felt encouraged by the survivors with whom I spoke, and their families. I also needed to try to make sense of the small group of vocal survivors in this debate. Was I getting a sample bias? Did this small group of survivors have the right to speak for *all* survivors? How should I interpret the silence of the survivors who have not spoken? Should I give the fact of their silence any special moral weight? What about those survivors who disagree?

Another limitation of my project concerns its binary approach. For simplicity's sake, I divide the debate into survivors on one hand, and medical ethicists and researchers on the other—suggesting no overlap. But certainly we find a few survivors on the other side, and some medical ethicists and researchers support the survivors' claims. Nonetheless, the fact remains that the survivors' many claims, the ones that I have mentioned, have heretofore been largely dismissed. I needed to make sense of *these* claims, realizing of course that *not all* survivors make these claims, and *not only* survivors make these claims.

I am confronted with what I call "Frankl's Challenge," which is a challenge to any "outsider" to some tragic event that they have nothing important to contribute to our collective understanding of the event or ourselves. In his work, *Man's Search for Meaning*, survivor Viktor Frankl claims that to attempt a methodological presentation of this subject is very difficult, since it requires a certain detachment. "Such detachment is granted to the outsider, but he is too far removed to make any statements of real value."[1] I accept Frankl's challenge and hope that there is some measure of value in my labor.

NOTE

1. Victor Frankl, *Man's Search for Meaning* (New York: Simon and Schuster, 1959), 24.

Acknowledgments

Various kinds of support eased the writing of this book. I could never have completed this work without the loving support of my family, friends, and my many mentors, including Bogdan Chlebus, Michael and Judy Quinn, Patrick Quinn, Randall Sunshine, Sean McAleer, Don Mather, Samuel Gorovitz, Linda Martín Alcoff, Tamar Gendler, Lynne McFall, Laurence Thomas, and the late Claudia Card. Thanks to Provost Vicki Golich and Dean Joan Foster for providing sabbatical support so that I could dedicate time to completing this project. Thanks to my student John Wilhelm who assisted me in understanding standpoint epistemology's roots in literary realism (chapter 6) and Sean McAleer who provided extensive comments on chapter 5. Thanks to Syracuse University faculty and graduate students for also offering helpful feedback on chapter 5, which I presented at one of their 2016 colloquiums. Thanks to anonymous reviewers for providing extremely valuable suggestions on previous drafts, many of which were incorporated into this work. Many insights in this book would not have been possible without the various conversations I had with survivors and their families on a 2000 trip to Israel, supported in part by a grant from the DOROT foundation. Finally, several audiences provided stimulating questions, comments, advice, and support.

Parts of chapters draw on work begun in my dissertation and in short articles, especially "Towards a Social Conception of Dignity," *The International Journal of Applied Philosophy* 22, no. 1 (2008). The material has been significantly revised, rethought in the context of theories developed in this book, and greatly expanded with new material.

Introduction

During World War II, Nazis conducted torturous and often deadly medical experiments on concentration camp inmates. The experiments received public attention as a result of the Nuremberg Trial conducted by Allied Forces after the war, at which twenty-three Nazi doctors and scientists were tried for war crimes and crimes against humanity. Although in many cases the Nazi medical data is considered to be worthless, some of the experiments (especially the Dachau immersion-hypothermia experiments) are believed to have produced useful results. Indeed, in North America, the uncritical use of Nazi data continued unchallenged until the late eighties, at which time an international conference was organized on the ethics of using the data, held in May 1989 at the Center for Bioethics at the University of Minnesota. So far as I am aware, there has not been another conference of this kind since. The decision to do nothing (with the exception of a few reputable journals that have decided not to publish articles that cite Nazi data, and the Environmental Protection Agency's decision not to cite the data in their report) has kept everything status quo. Researchers, protected under the First Amendment, continue to make use of unethically obtained data, including Nazi data.

US physiologist and hypothermia expert, Robert Pozos, who helped organize the conference with the Center for Bioethics' then-director, Arthur Caplan, explained that the conference would have a balanced representation of all interested parties. As he described it, "Invitations have been given to individuals from scientific backgrounds, ethics experts, and leaders of concerned parties (Jewish community leaders, for example). It is of critical importance to me that the conference be directed with professionality and sensitivity."[1]

Significantly, survivors of Nazi medical experiments were not among those Pozos listed as important contributors to the debate, although some did attend. We can get a sense of how they were treated by considering the following statement made by a clearly frustrated survivor, Susan (Sara) Vigorito, who had been sitting in the audience: "I have been in this room for two days. Everyone has spoken about data, data, data. It's the most sterile word. You are looking at the data, the living data, of Dr. Mengele. This is the data. It is my experience."[2]

From this statement, we can readily reconstruct what had been happening over the previous two days at the conference. First, the debate had largely been an impersonal, "sterile," scientific discussion, seemingly devoid of passion or concern for the victims. Second, the survivors had not had much voice in the debate. Indeed, when survivors did speak, they were largely ignored or dismissed. For example, one audience member told a survivor that she was an "emotional cripple," "ruled by emotions and not by the mind," and therefore unqualified to participate in the debate.[3] Sadly, we should not be surprised by this audience member's reaction, given the attitudes toward trauma survivors at that time—attitudes that still persist to this day.

Myra Giberovitch is a social worker who works with Holocaust survivors. She is also a child of survivors. She was born in a displaced persons camp at the end of World War II and grew up in Israel and Montreal. As she explains, the clinical research literature of the 1960s through 1980s promoted negative perceptions of Holocaust survivors as emotionally and mentally crippled people unable to function normally. The "concentration camp survivor syndrome" that emerged during this time stereotyped and stigmatized thousands of survivors as "dysfunctional victims."[4] Before we continue, it would be good to pause and briefly review the history of the mental health profession's relationship to Holocaust survivors.

Psychologist Natan Kellermann (also a child of Holocaust survivors) notes that "The psychological assessment of Holocaust survivors has a rich and varied past and has continued in intervals almost since the release of the first emaciated camp inmates."[5] Kellermann identifies major historical milestones in this research, including Leo Eitinger's pioneering work, *Mortality and Morbidity after Excessive Stress* (1973), which argues that the severity of the survivors' mental disorder (concentration camp survivor syndrome) was "correlated with the severity and duration of the concentration camp experiences, and not related to the patient's organic or premorbid personality."[6] As Kellermann explains, this was a revolutionary idea at a time when chronic psychiatric disorders were thought to be the result of a "tainted" personality and disposition, rather than excessive stress.[7] Sparked by Eitinger's work, research on Holocaust survivors has continued uninterrupted throughout the world and with increasing intensity, giving rise to a detrimental view of survivors as emotional cripples. To be sure, this negative view has met frequent criticism for being based on "nonrepresentative clinical case reports, with an overemphasis on psychopathology."[8]

The psychopathology of Holocaust survivors continues to be a controversial topic. For example, Kellermann, citing pioneer trauma psychologist Judith Herman, notes that any statement describing survivors as disturbed evokes intense protest by this group, since it stigmatizes often already-disempowered people.[9] In the past twenty years, mental health professionals have started to advocate diagnosing Holocaust survivors with post-traumatic stress disorder (PTSD) and other mental health diagnoses, in order for their treatments to be covered by public health care.[10]

So-called experts in the debate whether to use Nazi medical data (the researchers and medical ethicists) have assumed that they, and not the survivors, have the right to decide what should be done with the data (because they are more intelligent, better educated, or more "rational"?); however, survivors are not willing to be regarded as having impaired judgment in this case. Instead, survivors call themselves the *real* moral experts in this debate:

> The credibility of eyewitness statements on this topic of the Holocaust has come to be questioned at a rising rate of frequency. Often the survivor is presumed to be an emotional cripple tied to the loyalties of past horrors and unable to make credible judgments concerning his or her experiences. Yet those of us who have lived and by chance survived the heinous tortures called experiments by the Nazis have a clearer understanding of the Absolute Evil of the Nazi doctor.[11]

Survivors suggest that since the so-called experts do not have direct access to the evil, they cannot properly understand the debate, and so they do not have a right to say whether the data should be used. Researchers have always assumed that they have the right to use the data, but this is a mistake.

Vigorito was housed for over one year (until liberation of the camp) with her twin sister Hannah in a wooden cage one and a half yards wide in Josef Mengele's private laboratory. As Vigorito describes it, Mengele would repeatedly scrape, without anesthetic, at the bone tissue of one of her legs. Hannah died as the Soviets arrived at the gates of Auschwitz from repeated injections of an unknown substance into her spinal column. Vigorito states, "Only the survivors have the right to decide what should be done with the Nazi research. I have a clearer sense of the evil behind the data than you do."[12] And in response to the claim that she was at a disadvantage because she had been in Auschwitz and so was ruled by her emotions, Vigorito replied, "Experience is the best education."[13]

Most survivors (and their supporters) who have opposed the data's use, and especially without the survivors' consent, suggest that using the data harms them: "Use of the data amounts to the victims' final indignity";[14] "We would dishonor the victims once more by feasting on their bodies";[15] "To use the data without the consent of those who were violated is to violate the violated anew."[16] In this work, I argue that the survivors (or if they are deceased, their family members or other surrogates) should control the data, so that it should be *for them* to decide what should be done with it, whether or not it should be used. Specifically, I argue that the survivors should control the data because (1) they are the "living data"; (2) controlling the data will help restore their dignity rather than further degrade it; (3) we should care about their well-being; and (4) they know best what to do with the data, since they are the moral experts in this debate.

In defending the reason that it should be for the survivors (or their surrogates) to control the data, I motivate two, sometimes intertwining, concerns. The first concerns doing what is right by the survivors. To this end, I argue that since the data is a part of the survivors' selves, and one should have control over one's self as a matter of dignity, then in the interest of restoring the survivors' dignity they should control the data. This concern constitutes the bulk of the arguments in this work, since I am foremost concerned with the survivors' well-being and to do well by them.

The second concerns doing what is right for our community and its future, and is thus motivated by consideration for its well-being. Here the survivors' moral expertise comes into play. By virtue of their experiences, because the data is a part of their selves and so they know it most intimately, survivors are the true moral experts in the debate. The survivors alone properly understand that the data *itself* is saturated in evil—an evil that continues to taint all who engage it. We should therefore defer to the survivors' judgment concerning what is best for our community and not use the data.

Underlying my approach is a desire to defend an ethics of honoring and deferring to the testimonies, experiences, and wishes of victims of unethical experiments and indeed of atrocities of all sorts. I promote this ethics against what I call the "cool-headed rationalism" that disparages the emotionally charged claims and experiences of those still often haunted by a traumatic past. That ethics seems all too willing to downplay or outright ignore the well-being of victims for the sake of knowledge at all costs. This work thus serves to help undermine this morally flawed logic.

In "Bearing Witness or the Vicissitudes of Listening," Dori Laub writes about his experience at a professional conference in which academic historians, with their rigid adherence to historical "facts," callously dismissed an experience-based account of an Auschwitz survivor. Conference participants watched the videotaped testimony of the woman narrating her experience. As Laub notes, "A lively debate ensued. The testimony was not accurate, historians claimed. The number of chimneys was misrepresented. Historically, only one was blown up, not all four. Since the memory of the testifying woman turned out to be, in this way, fallible, one could not accept—nor give credence to—her whole account of events."[17]

The historians' remarks speak to the so-called false memory syndrome and the ways in which it has contributed to the survivors' disempowerment. False memory syndrome is based on mistaken beliefs about the efficacy of memory, and our misplaced understandings of how memory, and in particular *trauma memory*, works. Victoria L. Banyard discusses what she calls a "major debate" in the trauma field concerning the nature of memories about traumatic events. The debate is at times divisive in its tone, "with trauma survivors and the clinicians who work with them expressing real concerns about the silencing of survivor's experiences."[18] The divisive nature of this debate is rooted in historically conflicting understandings of how trauma memory works. Traditionally, such memories were believed to be fixed and inflexible. As Sharon Dekel and George Bonanno note, "the arousing nature of the event was thought to create long-lasting memories that are relatively immune to change over time. In recent years, this so-called static notion of trauma memory has been seriously challenged."[19] It turns out that *all* memory, not exclusively trauma memory, is by nature imperfect, constructive, and subject to change over time.[20] Michele Bedard-Gilligan et al. explain how trauma memories are now believed to work. Trauma narratives are "characterized by sensory aspects, incoherence, and a lack of sequence, collectively referred to as 'fragmentation.'"[21] As they note, the fragmented nature of trauma narratives becomes more organized over the course of treatment. Therapists who treat trauma survivors often cite this as part of their rationale for treatment.

On Laub's accounting of the conference he attended, the historians argued that since the survivor did not know the number of chimneys that blew up, she knew nothing.[22] Unsettled by what had transpired at the conference, Laub devoted himself to defending the validity of testimony and developing a theory of experience-based historical knowledge. Due in large part to the important work of people like Laub, the commitment to honor victims' testimonies and traumatic experiences has become central to recent Holocaust and trauma studies.

My project follows this tradition. In chapter 1, I provide a brief overview of the debate, ending with a discussion of the main arguments for and against using the Nazi medical data. In chapter 2, I lay the groundwork for chapter 3 where I defend an alternative conception of dignity that best captures survivors' claims of harm. I present Immanuel Kant's account of dignity, since his is one of the earliest and most influential conceptions, certainly among philosophers. Showing how Kant's account fails to capture the survivors' claims of harm lays bare the need to arrive at an adequate conception. In chapter 3, I consider what I call the survivors' "argument from dignity." Here we run into some conceptual difficulty, because the term that seems best to describe their claims of harm is "dignity" (and, indeed, many survivors use this word in the literature), yet when I talked with survivors on my trip to Israel, I was told that the proper word is not "dignity" but *kavod* (כָּבוֹד). It turns out that *kavod* is similar to the alternative (social) conception of dignity that I propose, and so perhaps it is just a matter of calling what I propose by a different name. I provide a conception of dignity (or *kavod*) that requires (1) control in the sense of self-determination; (2) societal acknowledgment of value; (3) living a life worthy of pursuit (that is, engaging in worthy life projects); and (4) acting morally responsibly.

Once we understand the requirements of dignity/*kavod*, we should have no trouble seeing that the survivors' healing requires regaining the control that they lost in the camps. This can be accomplished by engaging in worthy life projects, thereby gaining the acknowledgment and respect of the community. J. M. Bernstein similarly understands that "If dignity is a social construction whereby a group bestows on its members the status of possessing intrinsic worth, then it can only survive, finally, in a community capable of upholding relations of mutual recognition at some fundamental level."[23]

The survivors want to prevent future atrocities and make the community a better place. This is a worthy life goal. The proliferation of Holocaust memoirs and other writings suggests the large number of survivors who have worked toward this end of prevention. Working toward this end is an important step in their healing process, as psychologists of trauma teach us. In the case of survivors of Nazi experiments, I argue that their life projects concern preventing another medical atrocity. We clearly see this in their writings and testimony. They strongly believe that prevention is connected with what we do with the data and they alone (because they are the living data; because they are the *real* moral experts in the debate) have the right to decide what should be done with it. On the survivors' view, preventing them from having control of the data (using the data without their consent), counts as a harm by preventing them from engaging in this worthy life goal.

In chapter 4, I draw on the insights of trauma pioneers Judith Herman and Ronnie Janoff-Bulman, as well as contemporary research in trauma studies, to discuss how trauma affects the self (by rendering the victims out of control) and how recovery from trauma specifically requires regaining control. I argue that we should give survivors control of the data (that is, of the data's use), because in giving them control we help them heal from an ongoing harm—and not merely the harm that originated in the camps. While the survivors have not, to my knowledge, articulated this suggestion, it meshes well with current psychological thought about trauma and healing from trauma and is compatible with other claims that the survivors make.

I argue that the survivors have been subjected to a *triple indignity*. First, they underwent torturous medical experiments without their consent; second, we robbed them of control of the data despite their protests (and in so doing we continue to use them); and third, we undermined their humanity by callously dismissing them as "emotional cripples" at the 1989 conference (of course I do not mean to suggest every participant). I witnessed a similar dismissal over a decade later at a lecture I gave at the University of Haifa. As we will see, these last-mentioned are clear cases of epistemic injustice, which occur when a speaker is harmed in her capacity as a knower. This constitutes not merely an epistemic harm, but one that threatens to undermine the speaker's very humanity.

Another reason that survivors give for their right to control the data is that their experiences have put them in an epistemic advantage with respect to the debate, and so they know what is best for the well-being of our community and its future. One of their insights is that the data is evil—not merely symbolically, but *truly* evil—and we continue to harm ourselves and our community when we use it. In order to make sense of these claims, we must arrive at a conception of the self and its relationship to cultural objects that best explains the survivors' (and our) relationship to the Nazi data. In chapter 5, I suggest a phenomenological approach, drawing on the insights of Maurice Merleau-Ponty. I also invoke research on intergenerational trauma by trauma specialists Rachel Yehuda and others to further support my claims in this chapter, and I discuss specific ways that researchers can be harmed by engaging the data, drawing on research on vicarious traumatization.

Recall that Vigorito refers to herself as the living data of Dr. Mengele. By referring to herself thusly, she suggests that when we use the data (and especially without her consent) we ipso facto use her. I defend this claim, arguing that the survivors are right when they state that we harm them, and their experiences give them this insight. But we also harm our community and ourselves. This last claim is especially important, since this suggests that even after all of the survivors are gone, we perpetuate harm so long as we continue to use the data. This becomes clearer once we understand that the survivors' children and grandchildren often share the grief and terror of their traumatized parents and grandparents.[24]

Over the past few decades, greater than five hundred papers have been published on the transmission of Holocaust trauma from the survivors to their offspring. Notably, their children's problems are rooted in the self and impaired self-esteem, among other problems.[25] Hadas Wiseman et al. discuss the so-called conspiracy of silence, which refers to a nonverbal spoken agreement in the family to keep some traumatic experiences unspoken and detached from everyday life. As they note, this may have major consequences for Holocaust offspring's inner and interpersonal lives. Further, offspring are prone to feelings of survivor guilt on two counts: (1) the parents' feelings of guilt may have been transmitted to their children, and (2) the children may feel guilty toward their parents because of their parents' suffering, even though they are not responsible for it.[26] As we will see, this connects with my conceptions of dignity and harm. Further, when we use the data, we harm the entire Jewish people, many of whom have never fully recovered from this tragedy. This is felt foremost in Israel, where the Holocaust is "a living catastrophe for the entire nation."[27]

In chapter 6, I discuss how dismissing survivors as emotional cripples counts as a paradigmatic case of what Miranda Fricker and others call "epistemic injustice." I argue that, far from being emotional cripples, survivors are the *real* moral experts in the debate, drawing on the work of standpoint epistemologists. I also engage those who are suspicious of knowledge by testimony and moral expertise generally. Of course, experts of any kind are by no means infallible. However, if survivors are indeed the experts then we ought to pay serious attention to what they say.

NOTES

1. Robert Pozos, Letter to Dr. Judith Bellin, US EPA document (August 2, 1988).
2. Susan Vigorito, *Long Island Jewish World Newsletter* (July 4, 1989).
3. See Robert Leiter, *Long Island Jewish World Newsletter* (July 4, 1989).
4. Myra Giberovitch, *Recovering from Genocidal Trauma: An Information and Practice Guide for Working with Holocaust Survivors* (Toronto: University of Toronto Press, 2014), 51, 53.
5. Natan P. F. Kellermann, *Holocaust Trauma: Psychological Effects and Treatment* (New York: iUniverse Inc., 2009), 24.
6. *Ibid.*, 25.
7. *Ibid.*
8. *Ibid.*, 27.
9. *Ibid.*
10. *Ibid.*, 35.
11. Susan Vigorito, "Far from Emotional Cripples, We Survivors of the Holocaust Have a Clearer Understanding," *Cleveland Jewish News*, May 26, 1989.
12. Robert Leiter, *Long Island Jewish World Newsletter*, July 4, 1989.
13. *Ibid.*
14. Isabel Wilkerson, "Nazi Data and Ethics of Today," *New York Times,* May 21, 1989.
15. Jay Katz, *Long Island Jewish World Newsletter*, July 4, 1989.
16. Stephen Post, "The Echo of Nuremberg: Nazi Data and Ethics," *Journal of Medical Ethics* 17 (1991): 42.
17. Dori Laub, "Bearing Witness or the Vicissitudes of Listening," in Shoshana Felman and Dori Laub, *Testimony: Crisis of Witnessing in Literature, Psychoanalysis, and History* (New York: Routledge, 1992), 59–60.

18. Victoria L. Banyard, "Trauma and Memory," *PTSD Research Quarterly* 11, no. 4 (Fall 2000), at ptsd.va.gov.

19. Sharon Dekel and George Bonanno, "Changes in Trauma Memory: Patterns of Posttraumatic Stress," *Psychological Trauma: Theory, Research, Practice and Policy* 5, no. 1 (2013): 26–34.

20. Victoria L. Banyard, "Trauma and Memory," *PTSD Research Quarterly* 11, no. 4 (Fall 2000), at ptsd.va.gov.

21. Michele Bedard, et al., "Is Trauma Memory Special? Trauma Narrative Fragmentation in PTSD: Effects of Treatment and Response," *Clinical Psychological Science* (March 2017).

22. Laub, 63.

23. J. M. Bernstein, *Torture and Dignity: An Essay on Moral Injury* (Chicago: University of Chicago Press, 2015), 288.

24. Natan P. F. Kellermann, *Holocaust Trauma: Psychological Effects and Treatment* (New York: iUniverse Inc., 2009), 70, 95.

25. *Ibid.*, 73. See also Kellermann, "Transmission of Holocaust Trauma—An Integrative View," *Psychiatry* 64, no. 3 (2001): 256–67.

26. Hadas Wiseman, et al., "Anger, Guilt, and Intergenerational Communication of Trauma in the Interpersonal Narratives of Second Generation Holocaust Survivors," *American Journal of Orthopsychiatry* 76, no. 2 (2006): 176–7.

27. *Ibid.*, 106.

Chapter 1

An Overview of the Debate

In order to situate our debate in its historical context, let us begin by considering the motivations for the Nazi medical experiments. Many experiments were conducted for the benefit of the German war effort. These included high-altitude studies, sea water experiments, malaria vaccine trials, and immersion-hypothermia experiments conducted at Dachau; mustard gas and phosphorus burn experiments conducted at Sachsenhausen, Natzweiler, and other camps; and typhus vaccine trials conducted at Buchenwald and Natzweiler. Some experiments were pseudoscientific, little more than crudely conceived exercises in torture, lacking scientific design, and poorly executed. In some cases, the evidence was obviously fabricated, and in others the experiments were pornographic. For example, female and male prisoners were sometimes forced to have sex with each other. In the Dachau immersion-hypothermia experiments, this method was tried as a "rewarming" technique.[1] The Chief Counsel for War Crimes at the Nuremberg Trial explained that "in every one of the experiments the subjects experienced extreme pain or torture, and in most of them they suffered permanent injury, mutilations, or death, either as a direct result of the experiments or because of lack of adequate follow-up care."[2] Nazi medical personnel also performed nonexperimental medical crimes, including euthanasia and forced sterilization, and subjects were "operated on" for the sole purpose of training medical students and residents in surgical techniques.[3]

Many researchers, including US hypothermia expert Robert Pozos who helped organize the 1989 conference, consider the Dachau immersion-hypothermia data to be valuable. Indeed, Dachau scientists presented their findings at an October 1942 international conference entitled "Medical Questions in Marine and Winter Emergencies," attended by ninety-five physicians and scientists, including the most eminent in their field.

After the war, American soldiers discovered the Dachau documents. Leo Alexander, a major in the US Army Medical Corps and advisor to the Chief Counsel for War Crimes, evaluated the data and judged it to be valid. According to Alexander, "Dr. Rascher, although he wallowed in blood . . . and in obscenity, nevertheless appears to have settled the question about what to do for people in shock from exposure to the cold. The final report satisfies all the criteria of objective and accurate observation and interpretation."[4]

Alexander's report, "The Treatment of Shock from Prolonged Exposure to Cold, Especially in Water" (1945), has been cited in over 100 research articles (that number climbs into the thousands when we take into account researchers who have cited articles that cite Alexander's report). But the hypothermia data is not the only Nazi data considered to be valuable. According to Arthur Caplan, "Nazi data and the claims of Nazi science in areas such as genetics, physiology, pathology, anthropology, and psychiatry have in the past been studied, cited, and absorbed into mainstream science with little comment."[5]

Nazi medical data has been used in matters of national interest. The US space program, for example, used Nazi data and employed Nazi scientists to build its rocketry program. Nazi medical material has also been used as teaching aids at reputable universities worldwide. Only a few decades ago, body parts and complete cadavers of victims were used for study at several German medical schools, including Tübingen and Heidelberg. In Britain, medical schools used x-ray films of victims in motion. The doses of radiation used to produce the films were so considerable that victims most certainly died from their effects. Cambridge University discontinued using the films in the late 1980s, but only after new technology made them obsolete.[6]

In North America, researchers continued to use Nazi medical data with little remark until Pozos came across Alexander's report. As Pozos explains, he has immersed hundreds of volunteers in vats of icy water in his own hypothermia experiments, but for ethical reasons he cannot let a subject's temperature drop more than 3.6 degrees Fahrenheit. As a result, he must extrapolate from extremely limited data. Only the Nazis offered actual data on severely hypothermic subjects. Pozos faced an ethical dilemma and asked the medical ethics community for guidelines about using the data. The result was the May 1989 conference.

At about this same time, controversy over whether to use Nazi medical data erupted at the Environmental Protection Agency (EPA) when the data was included in an August 1987 draft report on the effects of phosgene gas. The experiments were described without any discussion of the unethical way in which they were conducted. Page 29 of the draft report simply reads:

> An experimental study on the acute toxicity of phosgene in humans was performed during World War II. Fearful of phosgene attacks by the Allies in

Africa, Heinrich Himmler ordered Dr. Bickenbach to experiment on humans in an effort to develop a means of protecting the Germans against phosgene poisoning. Experiments were performed on 40 prisoners to investigate the prophylactic effects of hexamethylenetetramine (HMT) administration prior to phosgene exposure. HMT was administered at a level of 0.06 g/kg body weight to 12 prisoners orally and 20 prisoners intravenously prior to inhalation exposure to phosgene.[7]

After considerable opposition from EPA staff, beginning with a March 15, 1988 letter addressed to then-EPA Administrator Lee Thomas, the agency organized an ad hoc committee on the use of unethically obtained human data. They decided to omit the Nazi data from their final report. The committee stated two major concerns. First, they feared that the EPA's use of the data might legitimize past and future unethical experiments. Second, they worried that use under some conditions (such as when the knowledge seemed indispensable) might result in a slippery slope.[8] These and other concerns have been raised in the debate concerning whether we should continue to use Nazi medical data.

I have come across many claims that unethically obtained human data is not likely to be scientifically useful, and so the question concerning whether we should continue to use the Nazi data is moot. That is, many people argue that questions concerning whether we should use the data are "non-starters," because the data is worthless. On this view, the debate is over since the data is unreliable, being the product of sloppy methodology and poorly designed experiments. The research is shoddy, conducted by unqualified persons. The data is thus incomplete, inconsistent, and probably freely fabricated.[9]

Robert Berger argues in this way. Many scholars who have read Berger's paper state that he has argued so persuasively that the debate has been settled. Berger states that what he takes to be the only data considered to be of any worth (namely, the Dachau hypothermia data) is worthless.[10] As Berger explains, Dachau head researcher Sigmund Rascher was unqualified. While true, Berger overlooks the fact that Rascher brought on two reputable scientists who directed the study, Holzlöhner and Finke, both considered to be experts in hypothermia, and their results were presented at the reputable international conference noted above. Against Berger's claims, Jay Katz and Pozos argue that the Dachau findings "either confirmed prior experimental data or produced new data that scientists in the West have considered valid and have cited in scientific journals in support of their own findings."[11] And, as we saw, the data continues to be cited, up to this very day.

Between 1933 and 1945, the German medical community published extensively, and they did little to conceal their source of the data. Much of the world knew of their experimental "subjects." According to Caplan,

> Much of the basis for the Nazi murder of Jews, Gypsies, and others lay in the work of internationally respected German scientists at a time when Germany was the most scientifically advanced country in the world. . . . Most of the world [now] believes that scientists and doctors who participated in horrifying experiments . . . were people "on the fringe" but I do not believe that the medical and scientific community was dragged kicking and screaming into the Holocaust.[12]

Half of German physicians belonged to the Nazi party because Nazi ideas of "racial hygiene" meshed with then-current scientific thought.[13] Reputable, mainstream, university-affiliated researchers conducted at least some of the experiments with the goal of obtaining scientifically valuable data, and they often met their objectives. As Caplan notes, many experts now believe that German scientists and doctors were enthusiastic supporters of euthanasia, "racial hygiene," and racial superiority, and they may have even provided the foundation for Nazi ideology.[14]

People who claim that the Nazi data debate is moot conflate two different but relevant distinctions. The distinction is not between valid and invalid data (between "good" and "garbage" data), but between used and unused data. Respected researchers have used (and continue to use, despite survivors' protests) Nazi data, believing it to be valuable. Whether these researchers are right or wrong in their assessment of the data is irrelevant. The valid/invalid controversy avoids the more important (and more general) question: Is it ever ethical to use data obtained in unethical ways and, most importantly, who should make such decisions? Who should decide what happens to the data? Who should have control? Various considerations, such as whether and how the data should be expunged from the literature, or future uses of it, or what should be done with the original documents themselves, or how to make distinctions between the various types of experiments and the ways we should approach them, only come into play *after* we decide who should have control. Survivors argue that *they* should be the ones who control the data since (1) they are the "living data"; (2) they understand the harm we perpetuate when we continue to use it; and (3) they are the real experts in the debate, and so they know best what to do with it.

The survivors' claims are quite emotionally charged. As a result, they are often not taken seriously and sometimes callously dismissed. So we find in our debate the posturing of "experts" against the "token" survivor, all too often known as the "emotional" or "hysterical" survivor, whose claims are either undervalued or underexplored. There are exceptions, of course, such as Stephen Post who sensitively argues from the perspective of the survivors' rights.[15]

My challenge is to try to make "reasonable" what is understandably presented with great emotion. This is sometimes difficult. In 1998, I spoke at an international bioethics conference in Japan on the importance of taking Holocaust survivors seriously. After my talk, an audience member challenged: "The survivors are irrational. Do they really believe that we shouldn't use the data, *even after it has been explained to them* that it would save lives?" We can hear the paternalism in his words. In response, I described one survivor who claimed that even if a family member were dying, he would still insist that we should not use the data.[16] Many in the audience responded with balking and displays of shock and disbelief.

Do we really want to make sense of *this* survivor's claim? Should we dismiss him as extreme and irrational? ("Surely he can't really mean *that*.") Let us try to make sense of what he is saying. In making this statement, the survivor suggests that there is some value more important than saving lives—even the life of a loved one. Most of us would agree, I think, that we should not allow the torture of an innocent, even if this were the only way to save someone else's life, including our loved one. Such a decision might give us pause, since most of us quite reasonably give more weight in moral deliberation to ourselves and those we care about.

Someone might object that there is a morally relevant difference in these two cases. In the Nazi case the harm has already occurred—it is over and done. In the case of torturing an innocent for the sake of saving another's life, the harm has not yet occurred. But what if the harm in the Nazi case *is not over and done*? Then it becomes less clear whether there *is* a morally relevant difference in these two cases. While we might not be persuaded by the survivor's claim, we can begin to see how what at first appeared to be extreme and irrational can be quite rational.

Benjamin Freedman states,

> Discussions on the question of the use of Nazi data are often infused with passion. This is understandable, natural, and appropriate, and the absence of passion . . . is disquieting. . . . There are conflicting pulls of sources both in emotion and in logic, on either side of the debate. Conflict introduces an asymmetry between reason and passion, for reason of its essence can adjudicate conflict as emotion of its essence cannot.[17]

This debate, especially by those who exaggerate the usefulness of the data at the expense of the victims, has stirred painful feelings, anger, and resentment in the survivors. The survivors' feelings are readily apparent in their comments. Presumably, this has led many to ignore the content of their message and focus instead on the emotional way in which it is presented. Sometimes this is understandable. Often the survivor appeals to our emotions and imagination rather than "rational" argument. Vigorito, for example, challenges researchers that the next time they consider using the data, they should picture their mothers or fathers floating in tanks of icy water.[18] While we can understand such an approach, it might lead others to take them less seriously in the debate. Researchers, after all, can similarly respond: "But imagine your child, lying frozen in the snow, tearfully begging you to use the Dachau hypothermia data, for otherwise she will die."

Let us consider the emotional intensity of the following survivor, who echoes other survivors in arguing that using the data without their consent harms them (their dignity/*kavod*). Notice that the survivor takes the data to be as much a part of the victims' selves as their hair, fat, skin, and teeth:

> In Auschwitz we were treated like a commodity; the hair was used for mattresses; the fat was used for soap; the skin for lampshades; the gold collected from the teeth of the dead went into the Nazi treasury, and many of us were used as guinea pigs. Today some doctors want to use the only thing left by these victims. They are like vultures waiting for the corpses to cool so they could devour every consumable part.[19]

Many people (certainly the "experts" in our debate) take "cool rationality" to be the best standpoint for inquiry and knowledge, including evaluative inquiry and knowledge.[20] Since the survivors' claims do not exhibit "cool rationality," they are dismissed as the rants of emotional cripples. To be sure, emotions can put us in a bad epistemic position to make judgments, such as when anger clouds our thinking, and certainly some survivors might have distorted judgments due to their traumatic past. The question is whether good judgments require doing away with emotions altogether, or whether having "correct" or "appropriate" (albeit strong) emotions can leave us in a good position to make proper evaluative judgments. Understood in this latter way, emotions can provide an important access to knowledge by (1) putting us in a cognitive position not otherwise accessible, and (2) focusing our attention on what truly matters. Martha Nussbaum writes similarly, invoking Aristotle's and other Greek philosophers' conception of emotion: "[They] all held that emotions are not simply blind surges of affect, recognized, and discriminated from one another, by their felt quality alone; rather, *they are discriminating responses closely connected with beliefs about how things are and what is important.*"[21]

Holocaust scholar Lawrence Langer notes that after Auschwitz the notion of dignity would never be the same.[22] By this he suggests that before Auschwitz our conception of dignity was theoretical, devoid of the richness of experience and emotion. But the victims are intimately familiar with dignity and its related notions in ways not captured by theory. Further, their strong emotional response to the data's use suggests just how much they care about the debate, how invested they are in the process and outcome. So too, their emotions suggest that there is something to care about, that something is at stake.

Some experiences seem to provide insight into what to do in that they bring to light morally relevant concerns not previously attended to or outright ignored by those who have not had similar experiences. Is being a victim of Nazi experiments such an experience? The survivors say it is. We must understand what the survivors bring to the debate in terms of introducing new ideas and criticizing old, inadequate thinking and practices. The survivors' emotional connection to their experiences reveals not only the evil of the Nazi data, but that we become morally tainted when we use it. Further, they see that the data is not merely a collection of "objective" findings, but a real part of the victims' selves—as real as any other body part.

Holocaust survivor Hanna F. tells her interviewers that she survived by sheer stupidity. As Langer describes it, the interviewers laugh deprecatingly at her and dismiss her comment, "overriding her voice with their own 'explanation'": she had a lot of guts. Hanna responds in frustration: "No, no, no, no; there were no guts; there was just sheer stupidity." The interviewers refuse to accept her explanation. No one thought to ask her how one survives through stupidity, "as if she made some senile remark too obviously irrelevant to warrant investigation."[23]

In her work, *Ethical Loneliness*, Jill Stauffer recounts watching Hanna F.'s taped interview and provides her own accounting and analysis: One of the interviewers called Hanna "plucky" for her actions that got her out of Auschwitz. Mishearing the interviewer and believing that she said "lucky," Hanna responded by clarifying that it was not luck, but sheer stupidity. When the interviewer attempted to correct her, Hanna tried to rectify the miscommunication, at which point another interviewer stood up, blocked the camera, and announced, "I am going to take your microphone," effectively ending the interview.[24]

Stauffer disputes Langer's assessment that one of the interviewers was deprecating. Rather, as she puts it, it was "more likely that she really wants to support Hanna's strength in pushing her way through situations that many did not survive."[25] Stauffer also questions whether the second interviewer was deprecating. However, she notes that, "either way, the outcome is that Hanna doesn't get heard at precisely the moment when she seems to be opening up the most. It is a scene of failed hearing."[26] Stauffer explains the failed hearing as one in which Hanna tells the story that *she* wants to tell, not the one that the interviewers want to hear: "Hanna's interviewers seem to want redemptive stories about the resilience of the human spirit and the drive to live against all odds. Because that is what they want, that is also what they hear."[27]

Seven years after her first testimony, Hanna F. was interviewed by Lawrence Langer and Dana Kline. She was finally able to explain what it means to survive by sheer stupidity. As Stauffer explains, "stupidity seems to mean, for her, a kind of unreflective resistance to what was impossible about the situation in Auschwitz."[28]

Was Hanna dismissed in the original interview because she was old? A woman? A survivor? Was she dismissed because she did not fulfill the interviewers' expectations? Perhaps all of these. Almost certainly, Hanna was dismissed because the interviewers were "educated" (in psychology; in trauma; it doesn't matter) and her claim did not "fit" their theory. Survivors, because they make claims that do not "fit" what counts as knowledge by those who are properly "pedigreed" and "credentialed," are consigned to what Lorraine Code calls "epistemic limbo."

I witnessed just this imbalance of power at a talk I gave at the University of Haifa, attended by academics and survivors. I was speaking about my alternative conception of dignity, which I believe makes sense of some of the survivors' claims. After my talk, one survivor stood up, shook his fist at the ceiling, and with great passion cried out, "Not dignity, *kavod*!" When I asked him about *kavod*, he was interrupted by an academic who told me that "dignity" is not a Hebrew word, but *kavod* is clearly not the right term either. After the survivor was chastened to sit down, several academics proceeded to have a conversation among themselves, ignoring the survivor. To be sure, perhaps he was not shut out because he was a survivor—or at least not intentionally so. But if we consider the various reasons that he might have been shut out—that he was a survivor, or a very old man, or a nonacademic—none speaks well of the group that shut him out.

The Haifa audience was no different from most other gatherings of "experts" in their fields. They were merely operating within the "normal" paradigm of epistemic arrogance. Contrast this discussion with a subsequent one I had with the survivor at his home, outside of the academic setting. Over coffee and in the company of his friend (another survivor from his home town of Brzezany, Poland) the three of us—Nathan, Menachem, and I—had a wonderful discussion about *kavod* (I discuss the details in the next chapter). It is shameful that this latter discussion could not be carried out in the larger public space of my talk, where others could (indeed, should) have benefited from it.

Many arguments have been made for and against using Nazi medical data, including the survivors' argument that using the data without their consent harms them, it harms their dignity/*kavod*. Their arguments have been largely ignored or (callously) dismissed and much of this work will try to defend this and other survivors' claims. The ongoing importance of this debate can be seen in an anecdote related by David Bogod, editor-in-chief of the journal *Anaesthesia*. Bogod provides what he calls "a very depressing vignette" at a

2004 conference he attended in which a keynote speaker, a senior naval doctor, lectured about immersion-related deaths and near drowning. The speaker cited the Nazi data on two slides, the second being displayed, as Bogod puts it, "for an inordinate length of time." The speaker did not preface his use of the data with any explanation of its origin other than that the data came from Dachau. As Bogod explains,

> I was taken aback by this unexpected and unwelcome intrusion into an otherwise erudite presentation, but was even more surprised by the reaction of the audience to these slides. There was none. At the time, I put this down to a natural and creditable reluctance to offend a keynote speaker, but this optimistic view was dashed by the very next slide, which showed a photograph of a pig immersed in water, an experiment carried out in order to confirm the Dachau data. The slide was greeted by an audible sharp intake of breath from the audience, followed by a relieved exhalation when the speaker explained that the animal was anaesthetized, "otherwise I could never get it into the water."[29]

Let us briefly consider some of the main arguments presented in the debate before I focus on the survivors' arguments. The citations come from the 1980s and 1990s, when the debate dominated discussion in the medical ethics and research communities. The primary argument for using the Nazi data is its life-saving potential. Further, many suggest that we would be "compounding human suffering, not easing it, by allowing others to die when they might be saved by the knowledge gained in the Nazi experiments."[30] Similarly, Benjamin Freedman writes, "The evil done by the Nazis would be compounded by adding another wrongdoing—failure to use the available knowledge to save lives."[31]

Implicit in these claims is a rejection of the suggestion that we could alleviate the survivors' suffering by choosing not to use the data (or by giving survivors control). Indeed, implicit in these claims is a belief that the survivors' suffering is over and done and we need only consider future victims who might benefit from the data. Of course those who make such claims could also believe that the beneficial consequences of using the data outweigh the survivors' suffering.

Supporters of the data's continued use often express ambivalence about promoting its use. Freedman, for example, distinguishes between his philosophical, or public stance, and his personal feelings: "The conclusions [that we should save future lives by using the Nazi data] are too analytical and rational. On the occasions I've spoken publicly I've performed OK, but when I left, I felt like shit."[32] Others make similar remarks: "Intellectually, I'm convinced my arguments are sound. But they have a kind of obscene edge. I feel polluted."[33] Velvl Greene summarizes his ambivalent feelings with this statement: "On Monday, Wednesday, and Friday I think that the data should be used. On the other days, I disagree."[34] John Hayward explains, "I don't want to use this data, but there is no other and will be no other in an ethical world. I rationalize it a little bit. But to not use it would be equally bad. I'm trying to make something constructive out of it. I use it with my guard up, but it's useful."[35] Finally, Pozos expresses that "the reluctant conclusion that I arrived at in the interest of potentially saving lives down the road still awakens me at 3:00 in the morning."[36]

Most survivors (at least those who have made their views known) and their advocates oppose the data's use, arguing that such use harms them: "Use of the data amounts to the victims' final indignity";[37] "We would dishonor the victims once more by feasting on their bodies";[38] "To use the data without the consent of those who were violated is to violate the violated anew."[39] By contrast, one survivor suggests that using the data "will affirm the value and dignity of men and women whom the Nazis treated like laboratory rats."[40] Importantly, the survivors demand that *they alone* have the right to decide what should be done with the data, not the researchers or medical ethicists.

According to another argument in the debate, the evil of the Nazi atrocities has infused the data, and so in using the data we become morally tainted by this contact. On this account, using the data "brings medicine in touch with the untouchable."[41] The data defile us. We are rendered morally unclean by its use. Post writes that "It is a moral intuition that such tainted goods, even if useful, are steeped in such a degree of moral failure that their use is a grave profanity under all circumstances."[42] As we have seen, some survivors argue in this way. Greene, on the other hand, argues that "It is not a question of tainted, immoral, or illegal data. It is rather tainted, immoral, and illegal humans who did the work—people very much like us."[43] Some further argue that by using the data we implicate ourselves in the Nazi crimes. As Willard Gaylin puts it, to use the tainted data "is to become an onlooker, and beyond that, an accomplice."[44]

Others argue that the Nazi data is a "good" that can be salvaged from the evil of the Nazi atrocities, and for this reason we should use it. As Brian Falkner and Arthur Hafner explain, "since our society so highly esteems an understanding of the physical universe some . . . argue that any such information is inherently valuable."[45] Accordingly, data is data regardless of its origin in the same way that, for example, mathematical proof is mathematical proof. This account offends the survivors by "ignoring the moral aspects of scientific procedure—even to insist that they are irrelevant."[46] Further, it rejects the survivors' claim that they are the "living data" of the Nazi experiments, and so when we use the data we use them.

Still others argue that in producing good consequences (saving lives by using the Nazi data), we can now judge the balance of evil to be less (while still admitting the enormity of the evil) than had the experiments not produced any good consequences. Here it is not that the evil of the Holocaust has actually diminished, but we can now say that there was some measure of goodness coming out of it. In other words, we redescribe the Holocaust in light of the discovery of the (useful) data. Arguing in this way, the world could never have said at the time of the Nazi medical experiments that there is any measure of goodness in the Holocaust. But after the soldiers discovered the data and Alexander judged it to be valid, we can now say that *some measure* of goodness has come out of this atrocity.

What survivors find so offensive about this argument is that it suggests that the Holocaust was not entirely evil. Further, some argue that by using the data we go so far as to legitimize the experiments: "Imagine that . . . the usage of this Nazi data is commonplace and universally accepted. Mengele and other physicians who became butchers of the Holocaust would be looked upon as legitimate members of their profession. There would be no rest for those who suffered and there would be no dignity for the six million."[47] Similarly, survivor Gisela Konopka explains that using the data "would symbolically condone the practice of reducing human beings to bugs to be crushed."[48] Notice that these two survivors also make an appeal to dignity in their claims. Survivors liken themselves to bugs (to be crushed), corpses (for vultures to consume), and experimental guinea pigs.

Some argue that we can use the Nazi data for its great utility (saving lives) while condemning the experiments that produce this data. But can we really? Let us turn to Robert Martin, who asks us to imagine a situation in which a person who displays in his home a lampshade made from the skin of Nazi victims nonetheless genuinely deplores Nazism.[49] Let us call this person "Larry." When asked why he would do such a thing, Larry explains that the lampshade is a perfectly good lampshade, so there is no reason why he shouldn't use it. Martin suggests that we would call Larry "pathologically insensitive" and an exhibitor of bad taste, but since he genuinely deplores Nazism, we would not call him immoral.

This does not seem right. We are asked to believe that Larry genuinely deplores Nazism, and yet most of us would find it virtually (if not entirely) impossible to do so. We simply cannot bring ourselves to believe that Larry is entirely sincere since, at the very least, he ignores the symbolic meaning associated with displaying the lampshade.

Few would deny that the victims whose skins were used to make lampshades were harmed by this treatment. The victims would not want to be remembered as mere objects, but as subjects. We are rightly disgusted by such treatment and would consider any person who displays such a lampshade in his or her home to be deeply morally defective. From the survivors' point of view, there is little difference between using the victims' skins for lampshades and using the Nazi data. Both are intimately connected to the victims' experiences. As I will argue, in both cases the victims are "present" in the objects or, alternatively, the objects are a part of the victims' selves (their selves extend to the objects). This seems obvious in the case of the lampshades, but recall that the survivors also claim that the data is just as much a part of the victims' selves as their hair, skin, fat, or teeth.

Those who make moral judgments based on the importance of the results would argue that there is a significant difference between using the victims' skins for lampshades and using the Nazi data. One is trivial (there is no good reason to have a lampshade made out of human skin), but the other has great utility: potentially saving lives. Thus they would regard as unethical the display of dried skin lampshades, but might view using the data as ethically justified. The survivors, however, make no distinction between these two cases. This is because the data's historical association, and especially its association with the survivors' experiences, is undeniable. The Nazi data has a meaning that goes beyond mere objective findings. Its meaning is not exhausted by reference to these descriptions, for implicit in the data is a history to which it is inextricably tied.

The victims were part of the larger Nazi project of treating certain people as objects. Many survivors probably knew people who died and whose skins were used to that end, and they probably saw tanned human skins piled high in the camps. Eva Mozes Kor writes about remembering "the huge chimneys, the smell of burned flesh, the shots, the blood taking, the endless tests in Mengele's labs, the rats, lice, and dead bodies that were everywhere."[50]

The data is also part of the victims' experiences. Certainly one should have control over one's experiences and even the telling of one's experiences. Kor powerfully states that if *she* had control of the data, she would shred it and put it into "a glass monument with the inscription underneath, 'No human guinea pigs again.'"[51]

The final argument we will consider concerns the data's performative function. We can make a statement by using, or refusing to use, the Nazi data. For example, as a society, we can make a statement about the enormity of the evil of the Holocaust. In this case, there are a couple of options. First, we can refuse to use the data. As Kathy Nolan explains, "even if the information was useful . . . one's refusal to bring it into our world makes a very profound statement about how wrong this was."[52] And Howard Spiro writes, "We need to express our revulsion at some activities even if that revulsion means losing something irreplaceable. I cannot agree that we honor the memory of the dead by 'learning' from experiments carried out on their bodies. We make them retrospective guinea pigs by a strained utilitarian argument."[53]

Second, we can use the data and footnote the atrocities. Pozos argues that "republishing the information and including a statement in the research report condemning the heinous way the data was gathered will make a more profound statement than hiding the information and not saving any lives."[54] One problem with making a statement in this way is that it dismisses the survivors' claim that by using the data we continue to harm them, or it suggests that the data's life-saving potential outweighs that harm. Further, it reduces the survivors' harm to a footnote, and they find this insulting. Greene argues that the data should be put "under the floodlights" and on "center stage," and instead of banning it, the data "should be exhumed, printed, and disseminated to every medical school in the world along with the methodology and the names of the doctors who did it, whether or not they were indicted, acquitted, or hanged."[55]

We might also want to make a statement about how seriously we are prepared to condemn future ethical violations. Arthur Schafer explains that when a society stigmatizes research that conscripts involuntary subjects, or which unethically exploits or injures subjects, an important part of what the society accomplishes is the promotion of an enhanced ethical awareness among the members of that society. Accordingly, every research project has a part in constructing the norms of what is acceptable or respectable in methodologies.[56] Of course, this is not a foolproof deterrent. Rather, the argument is that we must take responsibility for how our use of the data affects, reinforces, and so on, existing practices.

Marcia Angell, writing about editorial responsibility, gives three main reasons not to publish unethically obtained data. First, refusing to publish the data is likely to deter future unethical work, since publication is central to the reward system in scientific research, and no one would knowingly jeopardize the opportunity for publication. Second, refusing to publish this data serves as a notice to society that even scientists do not consider knowledge to be the ultimate good of society. Finally, refusing to publish this data protects, from erosion, the primacy of the research subject.[57]

Someone might ask whether the intention of the original actor should matter in our decision whether to continue to use the data. Is not there a difference between (1) using the data created by a sadist who tortures his victims merely to satisfy his sadistic pleasure, and (2) using the data created by a researcher who harms his experimental "subjects" to gain useful information (as Nazi scientists did)? According to the survivors, there is no difference in these two cases, since both fail to acknowledge the victims' humanity and leave the decision-making in the researchers' rather than the survivors' (or their surrogates') hands.

We have reviewed some of the main arguments in the debate concerning whether we should continue to use the Nazi data. But engaging in the debate at this step effectively shuts out one key claim, the survivors' claim, which has heretofore been ignored; namely, *that they alone should make such decisions*. In the next chapter, I lay the groundwork for my alternative conception of dignity. I present eighteenth-century philosopher Immanuel Kant's account of dignity, since he provides one of the earliest and most influential conceptions. Showing how Kant's account fails to capture the survivors' claims of harm lays bare the need to arrive at an adequate conception of dignity, which I present in chapter 3.

NOTES

1. Matthew Gwyther and Sean McConville, "Nazi Experiments: Can Good Come from Evil?" *London Observer*, November 19, 1989.
2. A. Mitscherlich and F. Mielke, *Doctor of Infamy: The Story of the Nazi Medical Crimes* (New York: Henry Schuman, 1949), xxv.
3. Matthew Gwyther and Sean McConville, "Nazi Experiments: Can Good Come from Evil?" *London Observer*, November 19, 1989.
4. *Ibid.*
5. Arthur Caplan, "The Meaning of the Holocaust for Bioethics," *Hastings Center Report* (July 1989): 2–3.
6. Matthew Gwyther and Sean McConville, "Nazi Experiments: Can Good Come from Evil?" *London Observer*, November 19, 1989.
7. Draft Report, US Environmental Protection Agency, 1987.
8. Matthew Gwyther and Sean McConville, "Nazi Experiments: Can Good Come from Evil?" *London Observer*, November 19, 1989.
9. David J. Bleich, "Using Data Obtained Through Immoral Experimentation," in *Medicine and Jewish Law*, Volume II, ed. Fred Rosner (Lanham, MD: Jason Aronson Inc., 1993), 143.
10. See Robert Berger, "Nazi Science—the Dachau Hypothermia Experiments," *The New England Journal of Medicine* (1990): 332.
11. Jay Katz and Robert Pozos, "The Dachau Hypothermia Study: An Ethical and Scientific Commentary," in *When Medicine Went Mad: Bioethics and the Holocaust*, ed. Arthur Caplan (Totowa, NJ: Humana Press, 1992), 113.
12. Quoted in Jim Fuller, "Holocaust Casts Lasting Shadows on Science," *Star Tribune*, May 18, 1989.
13. Robert Proctor, quoted in "Scientists Say Holocaust Should Have Taught That Science Alone Falls Short," *Star Tribune*, May 19, 1989.
14. Quoted in Mike Steele, "Conference Will Study Holocaust and Bioethics," *Star Tribune*, May 17, 1989.
15. Stephen Post, "The Echo of Nuremberg: Nazi Data and Ethics," *Journal of Medical Ethics* 17 (1991): 42.
16. See Barry Siegel, "Can Evil Beget Good?" *Los Angeles Times*, October 20, 1988.
17. Benjamin Freedman, "Moral Analysis and the Use of Nazi Experimental Results," in *When Medicine Went Mad: Bioethics and the Holocaust*, ed. Arthur Caplan (Totowa, NJ: Humana Press, 1992), 151–52.

18. Susan Vigorito, "Far from Emotional Cripples, We Survivors of the Holocaust Have a Clearer Understanding," *Cleveland Jewish News*, May 26, 1989.

19. Eva Mozes Kor, "Nazi Experiments as Viewed by a Survivor of Mengele's Experiments," in *When Medicine Went Mad: Bioethics and the Holocaust*, ed. Arthur Caplan (Totowa, NJ: Humana Press, 1992), 7.

20. See for example Michael Stocker and Elizabeth Hegeman, *Valuing Emotions* (Cambridge: Cambridge University Press, 1996), 91–92.

21. Martha Nussbaum, *Love's Knowledge: Essays on Philosophy and Literature* (Oxford: Oxford University Press, 1990), 41, my emphasis.

22. Lawrence Langer, "The Dilemma of Choice in the Death Camps," in *Holocaust: Religious and Philosophical Implications*, eds. John Roth and Michael Berenbaum (St. Paul, MN: Paragon House, 1989), 23.

23. Lawrence Langer, "Interpreting Survivors' Testimonies," in *Writing and the Holocaust*, ed. Berel Lang (New York: Holmes and Meier Publishers, 1984), 35.

24. Jill Stauffer, *Ethical Loneliness: The Injustice of Not Being Heard* (New York: Columbia University Press, 2015), 73.

25. *Ibid.*, 73–74.

26. *Ibid.*, 74.

27. *Ibid.*

28. *Ibid.*, 79.

29. David Bogod, "The Nazi Hypothermia Experiments: Forbidden Data," *Anaesthesia* 59, no. 12 (2004): 1155.

30. Marcia Angell, "The Nazi Hypothermia Experiments and Unethical Research Today," *New England Journal of Medicine* (1990): 1462.

31. Benjamin Freedman, quoted in "Scientists Say Holocaust Should Have Taught That Science Alone Falls Short," *Star Tribune*, May 19, 1989.

32. Matthew Gwyther and Sean McConville, "Nazi Experiments: Can Good Come from Evil?" *London Observer*, November 19, 1989.

33. *Ibid.*

34. Quoted in Faye Sholiton, "Scientific Community Wrestles with Using Tainted Data," *Cleveland Jewish News*, November 25, 1988.

35. Quoted in Kristine Moe, "Should the Nazi Research Data Be Cited?" *The Hastings Center Report* 14, no. 6 (1984): 5.

36. Quoted in Faye Sholiton, "Scientific Community Wrestles with Using Tainted Data," *Cleveland Jewish News*, November 25, 1988.

37. Isabel Wilkerson, "Nazi Data and Ethics of Today," *New York Times*, May 21, 1989.

38. Jay Katz, Untitled, *Long Island Jewish World Newsletter*, July 4, 1989.

39. Quoted in Stephen Post, "The Echo of Nuremberg: Nazi Data and Ethics," *Journal of Medical Ethics* 17 (1991): 42.

40. Anonymous, "Learning from a Failure of Western Culture," *Star Tribune*, May 25, 1988.

41. Quoted in Stephen Post, "The Echo of Nuremberg: Nazi Data and Ethics," *Journal of Medical Ethics* 17 (1991): 43.

42. Stephen Post, "The Echo of Nuremberg: Nazi Data and Ethics," *Journal of Medical Ethics* 17 (1991): 43.

43. Velvl Greene, "Can Scientists Use Information Derived from the Concentration Camps? Ancient Answers to New Questions," in *When Medicine Went Mad: Bioethics and the Holocaust*, ed. Arthur Caplan (Totowa, NJ: Humana Press, 1992), 69.

44. Willard Gaylin, "Commentary," *Hastings Center Report* (July–August 1989), 18.

45. "Case Studies: Nazi Data: Dissociation from Evil," *Hastings Center Report* 14, no. 4 (July–August 1989). "Commentary" by Falkner and Hafner.

46. Robert Martin, "Using Nazi Scientific Data," *Dialogue* XXV (1986): 408.

47. Anonymous, "Learning from a Failure of Western Culture," *Star Tribune*, May 25, 1988.

48. Gisela Konopka, "Holocaust Survivor Questions Data's Validity," *The Minnesota Daily*, July 27, 1988.

49. Robert Martin, "Using Nazi Scientific Data," *Dialogue* XXV (1986): 408.

50. Eva Mozes Kor, "Nazi Experiments as Viewed by a Survivor of Mengele's Experiments," in *When Medicine Went Mad: Bioethics and the Holocaust*, ed. Arthur Caplan (Totowa, NJ: Humana Press, 1992), 31.

51. Quoted in Matthew Gwyther and Sean McConville, "Nazi Experiments: Can Good Come from Evil?" *London Observer*, November 19, 1989.

52. Kathy Nolan, quoted in "When Research is Evil," *Minnesota Alumni Association* (November–December 1988).

53. Howard Spiro, "Nazi Research Too Evil to Cite," *Hastings Center Report* (August 1985), 31.

54. Robert Pozos, quoted in "When Research is Evil," *Minnesota Alumni Association* (November–December 1988).

55. Velvl Greene, "Can Scientists Use Information Derived from the Concentration Camps? Ancient Answers to New Questions," in *When Medicine Went Mad: Bioethics and the Holocaust*, ed. Arthur Caplan (Totowa, NJ: Humana Press, 1992), 69.

56. Arthur Schafer, "On Using the Nazi Data: The Case Against," *Dialogue* XXV (1986): 415.

57. See Marcia Angell, "Editorial Responsibility: Protecting Human Rights by Restricting Publication of Unethical Research," in *The Nazi Doctors and the Nuremberg Code: Human Rights in Human Experimentation*, eds. George Annas and Michael Grodin (Oxford: Oxford University Press, 1995).

Chapter 2

Kant's Conception of Dignity and How It Fails to Capture Survivors' Claims of Harm

Philosopher Sandra Harding writes,

> That these [Nazi] experiments should not have been conducted goes without saying and thus is not the issue raised in recent discussions. Nor is the issue whether to use the information, since knowing the "facts" produced through this "research" can help save lives. *The issue is whether and how the useful information thus produced should be cited in subsequent scientific reports.*[1]

Harding tells us that our debate does not concern whether to use the data (we should), but *how* we should cite it in future references. She does not discuss securing the survivors' consent before citing the data. She does not discuss the victims at all except implicitly suggesting that we ought to perhaps include them in a footnote as "torture victims" rather than "experimental subjects." That many survivors object to such use on the grounds that it harms them does not enter into Harding's discussion. Either she does not consider it important, or she might not be aware of the survivors' objections, and so perhaps she would not have said what she did had she been aware. In much of her writing, Harding advocates for taking marginalized voices seriously. Given this, I find it striking that she presumably did not consider the survivors in this debate or that the debate might include survivors' voices. This is all the more striking since Harding advocates engaging in research projects and promoting agendas from the perspectives of marginalized lives.

Survivors approach our debate from a distinct perspective. They suggest that using the data without their consent violates, reduces, or altogether destroys their dignity (I discuss the related notion, *kavod*, in chapter 3). I try to establish their claims by arguing the following. First, the victims lost a considerable amount, if not all, of their dignity in the camps. The question concerning just how much dignity the victims lost might sound strange to those who do not think of dignity as coming in degrees (Kantians fit this category). But if we think of dignity as directly related to control (in the sense of self-determination) and recognize that people exercise varying degrees of control, we can make sense of the claim that people possess varying degrees of dignity. Second, although many of the survivors of Nazi experiments have regained some measure of control since the trauma (and so some measure of dignity), they (or their family members or other surrogates) must control the data. Controlling the data further restores their dignity (even posthumously, in the continuation of their projects). Without such control, their dignity continues to be imperiled.

As presented, my argument is too sketchy to be convincing. To fill it in, I must (1) develop a conception of dignity connected with control which adequately captures survivors' claims of harm; (2) explain how trauma affects the self (it renders the victim out of control) and how recovery from trauma requires regaining control; (3) show how the survivors' recovery specifically requires controlling the data; and (4) describe how the survivors' dignity can be restored posthumously, in the continuation of their projects. While this last mentioned does not work toward the survivors' recovery per se since they are deceased, it does work toward community healing and healing survivors' descendants. This is especially relevant, since the remaining survivors are very old and will not be with us much longer.

Appeals to dignity are commonplace. People often appeal to dignity when they believe it to be threatened, such as when objecting to various dehumanizing or oppressive treatments. Appeals to dignity are frequently used in arguments for rhetorical force, but rhetoric often conceals a lack of understanding of this term. Some philosophers claim that it is not altogether obvious that the Holocaust victims lost their dignity in this atrocity. This suggests that while "dignity" is in common use among ethicists of various sorts, there is no agreed-upon definition of just what dignity is, although we all probably have a rough idea of what it means for some action to count as an offense to a person's dignity. But offenses to dignity are not the same as outright loss of dignity.

So as not to beg the question in favor of my account of dignity as requiring control, I appeal to our intuitions about whether the following narratives show that the Holocaust victims lost their dignity. In presenting these examples I do not want to suggest that *all* of the victims lost *all* of their dignity.[2] I do want to suggest, however, that what they experienced was considerably more than mere insults to dignity.

Auschwitz survivor Primo Levi writes about arriving at the camp. He and others were forced into a large, empty, poorly heated room. They had not had a drink for four days. Within the room is a tap that drips swamp water. Levi explains, "This is hell. . . . We are tired, standing on our feet, with a tap which drips while we cannot drink the water, and we wait for something which will certainly be terrible, and nothing happens, and nothing continues to happen."[3] He adds,

> Nothing belongs to us anymore; they have taken away our clothes, our shoes, even our hair; if we speak, they will not listen to us, and if they listen, they will not understand. They will even take away our name; and if we want to keep it, we will have to find ourselves the strength to do so, to manage somehow so that behind the name something of us, as we were, still remains.[4]

Survivor Frank Stiffel writes about the train ride to Treblinka:

> The car was hot; the air was foul. I could see a woman defecating directly under herself. A man urinated over another man, and an argument broke out between them. Mother said, "I'm thirsty," and I would have given my life for some water for her. . . . It wasn't a car full of Jews; it was Noah's ark all over again. Suddenly, these were not people but animals. Sick animals, dying animals, raging animals. The air of the slaughterhouse was all over us.[5]

Simon Wiesenthal writes about a little ghetto boy who swept up small bits of breadcrumbs left over for birds on a windowsill and brought them to his mouth.[6] Joseph Kirman tells a story about a father deeply saddened by his hatred of doves. The loaf of bread that the Nazis denied him to feed his child was hand-fed to cooing doves perched on frozen barbed wires.[7] People in the Warsaw ghetto consumed a mere 220 calories a day. Although food was occasionally smuggled into some of the ghettos, such opportunities did not exist at other ghettos like Lodz, where people were more quickly overcome by chronic starvation and disease.

Terrence Des Pres shares a story about inmates on death marches who could not even stop to relieve themselves in a nearby ditch: "Urine and excreta poured down the prisoners' legs, and by nightfall the excrement, which had frozen to our limbs, gave off its stench. We were really no longer human beings in the accepted sense. Not even animals, but putrefying corpses moving on two legs."[8]

Charles Reznikoff describes Jews who were part of the seawater experiments. The Nazis conducted these experiments because cases of distress at sea were multiplying due to intensification of air operations over the Mediterranean and Atlantic.[9] The airmen faced dying of dehydration. Experiments were designed to try to make seawater drinkable. The experimenters forced Jews to drink only seawater. Many Jews threw themselves on the mops and rags used by hospital attendants to try to drink the water clinging to them. In Reznikoff's *Holocaust* (a book composed solely of Holocaust survivor testimony and written in poem-like form), under a subheading entitled "Research," he writes that in their torment they

> sucked the dirty water out of them
> to quench the thirst
> driving them mad.[10]

According to the testimony of a Viennese medical student who was employed as a nurse for the Nazis, "Such patients, at times when they were left without supervision, quite often drank from sewage pails used by the nursing staff. . . . Some also, when the floor was washed, sucked up the water thrown over it."[11]

Just what is this dignity that survivors in these accounts (implicitly) suggest was taken from them? We need to find an adequate conception of dignity to capture their claims of harm. At first glance Kant serves as a likely source since, as Charles Taylor explains, he provides one of the earliest and most influential accounts of dignity, and his conception "has been the basis for our intuition of human dignity ever since."[12] Many philosophers take Kant to have given us an insightful way of thinking about this term. However, I suggest that when we study his account, it does not mesh with our ordinary intuitions about it. His conception fails to capture our ordinary talk (and even more so, *survivors'* ordinary talk) about dignity as something we can lose.

As Lawrence Langer explains, "We should at least be prepared to redefine . . . dignity . . . so that it conforms more closely to the way of being in places like Auschwitz.[13] By this he seems to suggest that people did not think to challenge the Kantian conception of dignity until the Holocaust forced us to rethink that term. Nietzsche was a notable exception. He said that our belief in human dignity was one of our "great errors."[14] Ruth Macklin similarly argues that dignity is a useless concept, meaning no more than respect for persons or their autonomy.[15]

We can best understand Kant's conception of dignity by contrasting it with other views he rejects. In what follows, I discuss seven important characteristics of Kantian dignity: (1) Dignity as moral worth; (2) Dignity as contrasted with contingent excellences; (3) Dignity is "intrinsic" rather than "instrumental"; (4) Dignity is an "unconditional" value, rather than a "conditional" one; (5) Dignity has a social element to it; (6) Dignity is grounded in autonomy; and (7) Responsibility is a consequence of dignity. I have benefited tremendously in conversations with the late Claudia Card and Joel Feinberg here.

1. *Dignity as moral worth, as contrasted with moral or individual merit of any kind.*

On Kant's view, moral worth attaches to all human beings by virtue of their humanity (and specifically, their rationality) whatever their merits or demerits.[16] In *The Doctrine of Virtue,* Kant tells us that the humanity in each person has dignity, no matter how immoral that person may be. He explains, "The censure of vice . . . must never break out into complete contempt and denial of all moral worth to the immoral man; for on this supposition he could never be improved, and this is not consistent with the Idea of man, who as such (as a moral being) can never lose all his disposition to the good."[17]

When Kant writes that we cannot deny all moral worth to the immoral man, this might suggest that we can deny him *some* moral worth due to his actions, but on his view a person's dignity does not diminish or increase according to what that person does. A murderer has just as much dignity as a virtuous person. As Kant explains, dignity does not depend on a person's moral achievements, but on her capacity as a moral agent. In other passages, Kant makes clear that a person's dignity consists precisely in her capacity to acknowledge, and place upon herself, the restraining force of moral law, a capacity attributed to all rational beings equally.[18] A person does not lose this capacity when she acts immorally. Although every person has this capacity, we do not always engage it.

Kant's suggestion that all people have the same capacity to acknowledge, and place upon themselves, the restraining force of moral law does not fit our experience. Some people, such as those who do not have a developed moral sense, seem to lack this capacity altogether. Does Kant work with an idealized conception of persons? In his *Observations on the Feeling of the Beautiful and Sublime,* Kant tells us that women avoid the wicked "not because it is unright, but because it is ugly. . . . Nothing of duty, nothing of compulsion, nothing of obligation! . . . I hardly believe that the fair sex is capable of principles."[19] Kant seems to imply that women altogether lack the capacity to acknowledge, and place upon themselves, the restraining force of moral law. But Kant continues, "I hope by that not to offend, for these are also extremely rare in the male." Perhaps Kant wants to say that women, like immoral people (or those less than "perfectly" moral) do not engage this capacity, because impulsions contrary to reason get in the way. Both men and women have the capacity, however only (some) men engage it.

What about those who are "deficient" in reasoning ability? How can they have such a capacity? Perhaps Kant uses "capacity" in the sense of "potentiality." To have the capacity to play the guitar is to have the ability to do so. I lack this ability, but I do have the potential to play (well, my guitar teacher might not think so). To have the potential to play the guitar is to be so constituted as to be able to develop the capacity to do so. We speak of a human fetus having the potential for rationality, by which we mean that it is the kind of thing that will become rational. The severely "intellectually disabled" and the five-year-old are both of the same kind, namely, things capable of rationality. However, in the first case, such a capacity will likely never develop.

On Kant's view, a person's moral merit, on the other hand, depends on whether her actions are done from duty, and not merely in accordance with it.[20] He tells us that a philanthropist who takes great pleasure in helping others does not have much moral merit if his actions arise out of his concern for others. By contrast, a person who is not particularly good-natured, having little sympathy for others, but who nonetheless acts beneficently because it is her duty, has a great deal of moral merit. This does not mean that the person who has moral merit must altogether lack feelings of sympathy or care, but it does mean that the person must not act from those feelings. The immoral person has little if any moral merit because she acts on maxims that cannot be universalized.

2. *Dignity as contrasted with contingent excellences.*
On Kant's view, dignity does not depend on our social position (as determined by race, class, gender, sexual orientation, etc.), our utility to others, and so forth. Kant is reacting to predecessors in the history of political theory. Before Kant's conception, only people of high social rank were said to have dignity. Our word "dignitary," a person of high or honorable rank, title, or office, still captures this notion. All other people lacked dignity and did not have civil rights equal to those who possessed it. Kant introduced a universal, egalitarian conception of dignity, according to which people of every social rank have it solely because they are human—or better, rational. Such a conception would serve as the ground for universal, equal civil rights.[21]

Although Kant never mentions "rights" in his *Groundwork*, his ethics helped pave the way for the belief in universal human rights. Kant's insistence that dignity is indestructible is meant to give universal grounds to the claim that offenses to dignity are always wrong, that such violations can never be justified. As J. M. Bernstein similarly notes, "The obvious basis on which individuals might lodge a claim that they deserve to have their human rights respected . . . that they have a right to have rights, is their possession of human dignity; to deny an individual her rights is to impugn her dignity, her intrinsic and equal worth with her fellow humans."[22] What is indestructible, then, is the right to be treated with respect, and the duty to obey that right, grounded in a person's intrinsic worth. Kant seems to promote, against the prevailing views of the time, that every person has intrinsic value and is thus deserving of rights.

During the Middle Ages, European Jews were depicted as satanic figures, for only the devil would kill the Christ, and they were denied all civil rights.

The Slave South of the United States viewed blacks as a subordinate, inferior class of beings who were therefore denied the rights of citizenship.[23] Christopher Stone states that "unless the rightless thing receives its rights, we cannot see it as anything but a thing for the use of 'us'—those who are holding rights at the time."[24] Such thinking has been common throughout history and motivates recent discussion in animal ethics. Until relatively recently, animals were not thought to have intrinsic value. They were only valued according to human needs and interests. Indeed, they are still viewed this way in many circles. Their value depended only on our valuing them. But some philosophers, Peter Singer for example, argue that animals—specifically those capable of suffering and experiencing enjoyment—have intrinsic value and rights because they possess their own needs and interests. For example, they have an interest in avoiding pain. Their rights, these ethicists argue, should affect our treatment of them regarding our diet, farming methods, experimental procedures, and so on.[25] The idea seems to be that without attributing value to a thing we lack strong enough reason to protect that thing and promote its flourishing, especially if we decide that we no longer value it.

Kant also believes that "all objects of inclination have only a conditioned value,"[26] and if not for people's inclinations, they would be valueless. On his view, things lacking dignity are not worthy of the concern of others. His redefining "dignity" with the idea that from such a notion follows that *all people* have civil rights—even the "pauper," the "idiot" (Kant's terms), and others not valued in society—is laudable and similar to the intuitions of those who support movements to confer rights on nonhuman things.

3. *Dignity is "intrinsic" rather than "instrumental."*
Kant explains that what has intrinsic value has value in itself, whether or not it is valued by anyone.[27] By contrast, something is instrumentally valuable if its value depends on our interest in it. What is intrinsic to a thing constitutes its essence. A person has dignity due to his humanity, which is his "proper nature" and makes him an "end in himself."[28] Kant tells us that "Man, and in general every rational being, exists as an end in himself, not merely as a means for arbitrary use by this or that will."[29] Human beings, unlike nonrational creatures, recognize the requirements of moral law, and this grounds their intrinsic value. They recognize that all persons are to be regarded as ends in themselves, and should never be treated as a mere means. Note that Kant does not object to using people as a means. When I go to a restaurant and the chef prepares my food, I am using her as a means to satisfy my hunger. But she is also using me as a means to help support her family. Kant is against using someone *merely* as a means. To treat someone merely as a means is to treat that person as a means, but not as an "end in himself." But what does that mean?

Kant tells us that we must treat humanity "never simply as a means, but always at the same time as an end."³⁰ He gives us two rules for treating others as persons. One is negative: we do not use others as a mere means. The second is positive: we must treat them as ends in themselves. Someone might suggest that treating someone as an end requires taking that person's interests into account and not overriding those interests for some greater good. We treat a person as a mere means, for example, when we employ that person in our sweatshop under horrific working conditions for abysmally low wages in the interest of making fancy running shoes. But we often override a person's interests for some "greater" good. Consider the business owner who is against relocating and fights the city planners who want to build a freeway through her store. In the end, the city's interests override the business owner's interest and she is forced to relocate, but we do not treat her as a mere means in this exchange. One major difference between these two examples is that we respectfully consider the business owner's interests, whereas we do not take into consideration the interests of the sweatshop employee.

Kant connects treating others as persons with the notion of consent. Consent is related to interests, since a person's consent usually reflects her interests. We treat someone as a mere means when we act on maxims to which no one could rationally consent. Kant does not require actual consent as a criterion for treating others as ends, but rather "hypothetical rational consent." What is the criterion for consent to be rational? We need only look at Kant's first formulation of his Categorical Imperative. It would be rational to consent to others treating me in certain ways only if the maxims of their actions could be willed universally. To universalize implies that I *in principle* get consent from others. If others would not consent to my maxims, such maxims cannot be universalized and so should not be acted on. For example, in discussing the wrongness of lying, Kant explains that "the man whom I seek to use for my own purposes by such a [false] promise cannot possibly agree with my way of behaving to him, and so cannot himself share the end of the action."³¹

While Bernstein rightly notes that "consent matters in the way it does because it is a social practice that protects, fosters, and elaborates essential aspects of autonomy, especially bodily autonomy,³² one problem with adopting the notion of consent as the criterion by which we judge whether someone is being treated as a person is that it is often unclear what constitutes consent. Does the sweatshop worker who does not quit her job because she needs the money to support her family consent to being treated in that way? It seems right to say that the sweatshop worker is (implicitly) coerced into working under such conditions, because her circumstances force her to choose this kind of work.

Marxists argue that the worker in capitalist society does not consent to her working conditions, because her situation demands that she cannot choose to be without work. During prosperous times she might be able to choose a better job, but she is still coerced since, unlike the wealthy in society, she cannot consent to nonemployment.[33] But just because a person's situation forces her to do something that she would not otherwise do, this does not necessarily constitute coercion. Consider my grandfather who abandoned his plans for graduate school to help support his mother after his father died. Is this coercive? It does not seem so. Another problem with adopting consent as a criterion is that it is not always clear what actions must be consented to in order for someone not to be treated as a mere means. Is the business owner, in our above example, being treated as a mere means just because she does not consent to relocating her business? It does not seem so.

To consent to something requires choosing to agree to it. Choosing to agree to something need not necessarily be tied to rational capacities except in a limited way. My dogs do not choose to agree to go on walks with me, unless wagging their tails constitutes consent (one of my dogs wags his tail when he is happy, nervous, or afraid, and so I cannot necessarily read his mood by his tail wagging). We limit talk of consent to people. Certainly people can agree to do something "without a thought"—that is, without exercising their rational capacities, such as my agreeing to meet a friend without thinking that I already had another appointment. Kant suggests that while consent is necessary for a person to be treated as an end, so is furthering the ends of others[34] which requires supporting others' rational capacities.

When Kant's speaks of a person's humanity, he is referring to her rationality, and when he talks about treating a person's humanity always as an end, we would hope that it would require acknowledging, developing, and engaging that person's rational capacities. On the other hand, treating a person as a mere means consists in damaging, obstructing, or failing to acknowledge that person's rational capacities. The sweatshop worker finds herself in an insufferable situation in which she cannot exercise her rational capacities. Indeed, her employer, in his treatment of her, does not even acknowledge her capacities, and for this reason she is not being treated as a person. By contrast, the business owner exercises her rational capacities, and her lack of consent to bulldozing her business does not count as her being treated as a mere thing.

4. *Dignity is an "unconditional" value rather than a "conditional" one.*
Kant reacts to Thomas Hobbes who identifies "dignity" with "price." To have a price is to have conditional value, and to be "above price" or "priceless" is to have unconditional value. In his *Leviathan*, Hobbes explains that "the public worth of a man, which is the value set on him by the commonwealth, is that which men most commonly call Dignity. . . . The value or Worth of a man, is as of all other things, his Price."[35]

Against Hobbes, Kant claims that human dignity is an unconditional and incomparable worth admitting of no equivalents.[36] Something is unconditionally valuable if its value does not depend on contingent facts like market price. As Kant explains, things have either a price or a dignity. If something has a price, something else can be put in its place as an equivalent. So if I put up my motorbike as collateral to take out a loan, the motorbike serves as an equivalent for the money, should I not be able to repay the loan. By contrast, human worth is "above all price,"[37] and since intrinsic moral worth is not based on any contingencies, its value is not subject to "fluctuations" in the manner of price.

On Kant's view, a thing with price can gain or lose value according to people's interest in it. Dignity, unlike price, cannot gain or lose value. People cannot gain or lose dignity, although they can certainly experience affronts to dignity. Since dignity is above all price, it can never be sacrificed for something of mere price—even happiness. Many of us are familiar with Ursula K. Le Guin's powerful short story, "The Ones Who Walk Away from Omelas." Omelas is a city of unbelievable happiness, which is only made possible by a child, naked and full of festering sores, being kept in perpetual filth, darkness, and misery, living on a half bowl of cornmeal and grease a day. Most of the citizens of Omelas, once they discover this truth, accept that this one injustice is worth their perpetual happiness. Kant would never allow the sacrifice of this child's dignity for the sake of the citizens' happiness.

Although Kant does not permit the sacrifice of dignity for something of price, does his account allow for the sacrifice of some dignity here for more dignity there?[38] Kant makes clear that dignity always outweighs price, but can ten thousand people's dignity outweigh one person's dignity such that it is morally permissible to sacrifice one person for the sake of ten thousand, or in the case of Tobias Wolff's *The Night in Question*, to sacrifice one's son for the sake of a trainload of people? This is particularly relevant to our debate where there are considerations of dignity on both sides: the dignity of the survivors, but also of future hypothermia victims in need of the data to save their lives.

According to Thomas Hill, allowing for some dignity to outweigh other dignity is *compatible* with Kant's claim that dignity always outweighs price. The problem, however, is that if we allow for such comparisons of dignity, Kant's account becomes little more than another version of utilitarianism, since moral decisions would be reduced to the weighing of "quantities" of dignity.[39] On Kant's view, dignity is a nonquantitative, non-scalar notion.

5. *Dignity has a social element to it.*
Dignity is an attribute, not merely of isolated individuals, but of persons as "ends in themselves," who are members of a moral community—a "kingdom

of ends."⁴⁰ Members legislate and are subject only to those laws that are universal in form ("Any person P in condition C must do X"). This view presupposes an ontological and epistemological "sameness" with an inherent indifference to people's circumstances. Kant asks us to abstract "from the personal differences between rational beings, and also from all the content of their private ends."⁴¹ We must disregard all distinguishing features of persons and make universal laws as if ignorant of our situations (something akin to John Rawls' veil of ignorance in *A Theory of Justice*). We must see each other only as rational beings, fully capable of legislating and obeying universal laws.

Kant suggests an equality that does not exist in "real life." The marginalized and disempowered—those who are in need of higher wages, better education, health insurance, family leave, child care, public transportation, retirement plans, even a roof over their heads and decent meals—do not make policy decisions, for example. People in power make decisions about social welfare, education, and medical care. But policymakers, social workers, administrators, and other "experts" often claim to know just how the disempowered feel, what they need, and how to solve their problems. Those in power presume to know just what policies the disempowered want, but often they operate from different value systems—for example, ones that emphasize self-sufficiency rather than community support. Policies, programs, and practices often do not work effectively, and sometimes fail miserably, because people's differences were not taken into account. For example, Western scientists have engaged in research projects for developing cheap, effective contraceptives as the solution to the "problem of overpopulation" among ethnic and racial minorities in the so-called Developed World, and Indigenous people of the so-called Developing World, without taking into account what they want: in most cases education, not contraception. In the United States, of those women who have been sterilized without their informed consent, a disproportionately large number has been African American.⁴²

Another problem with assuming that all people are equally autonomous is that often those in power blame the powerless for circumstances that are beyond their control. Helen Bequaert Holmes explains that "autonomy can be a dubious good for persons socially constructed as inferior because the concept of autonomy readily allows healthcare professionals to blame victims . . . by wrongly assuming that all persons have the resources of the idealized rights-bearer—a person of means untroubled by oppression."⁴³

A fundamental yet mistaken assumption people hold is that we can directly control what happens to us through our own behavior. We safeguard this assumption even in the face of contradictory evidence. Psychologists like Ronnie Janoff-Bulman teach us that "non-victims" often blame people who are in unfortunate situations. By blaming victims, we not only maintain the illusion of our own invulnerability, but we minimize our sense of responsibility for helping others. If we can convince ourselves that we are protected from adversity because of who we are and what we do, we can hold onto our belief in a just, non-random, controllable world.

This myth of control and self-sufficiency is particularly prevalent in the United States where people assume that anyone can make it in this "land of opportunity" (although people increasingly realize that this "dream" is out of reach for many). Here we regard victims as "losers" responsible for their own fates. People are less likely to help those they regard as blameworthy. In Buddhist culture, people are socialized to face and accept suffering and loss. In the United States, where this is absent, it is much easier to ignore the suffering of others, especially when we believe that people get what they deserve.[44]

To be fair, when Kant speaks of "legislation" in the *Groundwork*, he means "moral legislation" (that is, legislation of moral laws), not political legislation. Legislating in Kant's kingdom of ends is like legislating from John Rawls' original position, which is not a position from which one acts in the "real world" where inequalities exist, but a position from which one proposes the principles by which such acts are to be judged, with the knowledge that in the "real world" inequalities abound. Even so, by bringing inequalities to mind, I point to the continuing problem in Kant that he sees the noumenal self as having an autonomy that is not affected by the "real" world. On my understanding of the self, there is no such independence, no such equal autonomy, and even if there were, it would not be enough to ground human dignity—or so I argue. Similarly, John Jones writes that "by basing our dignity solely on reason and will . . . dignity pertains only to those features of us which are independent of the body. This is too narrow a basis for a conception of dignity, which is rooted in human existence as being in-the-world and which reflects the wholeness and totality of that existence."[45]

Although Kant's account puts people in a kingdom of ends, it is not sufficiently social, since it abstracts people from society, dislocating them from their situations. Further, on his view, people possess dignity independent of community, merely because they are human beings (qua "rational" beings). But "human being" is a biological and not a social category. Most importantly, Kant's transcendentalism regards experience as at most secondary and derivative of morality, which for him follows principles.

6. *Dignity is grounded in autonomy.*
Kant tells us that autonomy is "the ground of the dignity of human nature and of every rational nature."[46] Autonomy is a property of the will of every rational being.[47] Insofar as we can acknowledge and place upon ourselves the restraining force of moral law, we possess autonomy, which is to say, we are genuinely in command of ourselves.[48] When we ordinarily think of someone

being autonomous, we think of that person being free from undue social constraints, for example. We think of some people having more freedom than others. We take it to be an empirical fact that autonomy can be undermined or lost by social forces. Understood in this way, since autonomy is the ground of dignity and people vary in the amount of autonomy they possess, they must also vary in the degree of dignity. But Kant makes clear that all people have dignity equally.

Kant attributes autonomy on *a priori* grounds to all rational wills because of their rationality. All people have the capacity to recognize and follow the requirements of moral law. On his view, the political prisoner has just as much autonomy as the free citizen, although she has lost her civil rights. Kant takes autonomy to be "all or nothing." According to him, all rational wills have autonomy in two senses, one negative and one positive. First, the will is free "in respect of all laws of nature."[49] By this he means that when I make a decision, I choose among "open" possibilities—outcomes that are not determined by forces outside of my deliberation and choice. Second, the will is free in the sense of obeying only those moral laws it makes itself and which can become universal law.[50]

Kant argues that autonomy as a property of all rational wills cannot be proven, but is presupposed. "As the will of a rational being, it must be regarded by itself as free; the will of a rational being can be a will of his own only under the Idea of freedom, and as such a will must therefore . . . be attributed to all rational beings.[51] For example, when I talk about making things happen, my deciding to do this or that, I believe that *I* am the one doing these things. I do not suppose that a mad scientist is manipulating me. I act as if I am in control of my own thoughts and actions, and so for all practical purposes I am free. My freedom, and especially my freedom to make universal moral law, is the ground for my respect.

7. *Responsibility is a consequence of dignity.*
Kant discusses our duties to each other in a kingdom of ends. Responsibility is built into the notion of duty. For example, if I have a duty to pay taxes, then it is my responsibility to pay them. Kant explains that duty applies "to every member of the kingdom of ends and to all members equally."[52] Our responsibilities to each other include acknowledging "in a practical way the dignity of humanity in every other man," and to respect him "even though by his deed he makes himself unworthy of his humanity."[53] What might it mean, on Kant's view, to acknowledge the dignity of each person in a practical way? All people have rationality because of their humanity. This attribute gives us our dignity and makes us ends in ourselves. Acknowledging and respecting the dignity of others should include adopting policies and programs and developing resources that foster that rationality.

Members of a kingdom of ends should act responsibly. People do not always do this (indeed, some never do), but on Kant's view, not acting responsibly does not affect their dignity. The most morally irresponsible person has just as much dignity as the most morally responsible one.

Kant seems to present an improved conception of dignity over his predecessors by providing a justification for treating all people equally because of their shared humanity. However, his view cannot account for our ordinary talk (and certainly the survivors' talk) about dignity as something we can lose. A person cannot lose dignity on Kant's account. Yet Kant seems to suggest the opposite in the following: "[Dignity] cannot be brought into reckoning or comparison without, as it were, a profanation of its sanctity."[54] The key is to understand what Kant means by "profanation."

There are at least two ways to understand the word "profane." One definition is to treat a sacred thing with irreverence or disregard. This definition does not necessarily imply harm, for the sacred thing could be impervious to harm. A second definition of "profane" is to violate or pollute a sacred thing. This suggests harm. We cannot know what definition Kant had in mind simply by looking at this passage. Kant sometimes writes as if certain immoral acts destroy a person's dignity. Let us consider this passage: "By a lie a man throws away and, as it were, annihilates his dignity as a man.... He has even less worth than if he were a mere thing.... [He] makes himself a mere deceptive appearance of a man, and not man himself."[55] Perhaps since a person can annihilate her own dignity, and since members are interchangeable in a kingdom of ends, a person can annihilate others' dignity too. Of course a theory defending the interchangeability of persons can lead to troubling results. For example, Bernstein, discussing Hannah Arendt's *Origins of Totalitarianism*, states that Nazi practice and principle created the complete exchangeability and hence fungibility of all victims.[56]

Can we use Kant's conception of dignity to help survivors construct an argument against using the Nazi data? We must first consider the ways in which people might lose their dignity on Kant's conception. These include being treated as a mere means, being sacrificed, and being treated as something with a price. During the Holocaust, victims of the Dachau hypothermia experiments, for example, were used as a mere means for the preservation of downed Nazi pilots who, having parachuted into the freezing water of the North Sea, were victims of hypothermia. When we use the data, the suggestion might go, the survivors are being treated as a mere means for the preservation of present-day hypothermia victims. Of course this claim is not as obvious as the claim that they were used as a mere means during the experiments.

Perhaps we can try the following. In not treating the survivors' claims of harm seriously in our debate, or in outright ignoring or callously dismissing them, we treat survivors as a mere means, especially since we know that they do not consent to what we are doing and we certainly do not respectfully consider their interests. Or possibly better, the relevant consideration should be whether, if appropriately informed, the survivors *could* rationally consent. The answer is "no." This still does not get us what we want, for an overly sensitive person might think she is being harmed when she is not, and we do not necessarily treat her as a mere means in not taking her seriously. We must further show that our using the data counts as a harm, and that the survivors are therefore right in their complaint, and we are wrong in ignoring them. I will not develop this argument here. My present goal is to see whether Kant's account allows for the possibility of people losing dignity in the way that survivors claim.

Another way for the victims to lose dignity on Kant's account is if our using the data amounts to a sacrifice of them. Certainly the victims were sacrificed for the war effort. Rascher wrote to Himmler about the high-altitude experiments: "The experiments, in which the experimental subjects of course may die, would take place with my collaboration. They are absolutely essential for the research on high-altitude flying and cannot, as has been tried until now, be carried out on monkeys, because monkeys offer entirely different test conditions."[57] In standing as substitutes for monkeys, the victims were treated as things with price. While the victims were obviously mistreated in the experiments, it is more difficult to argue that we sacrifice them now when we use the data. Any adequate argument must show this, but we do not need to go that far for what I want to accomplish presently.

Although there are passages in Kant's writing that state that a person can lose dignity, such discussions directly contradict what he says about the immoral person elsewhere. For example, he explains, "I cannot withdraw at least the respect that belongs to him in his quality as a man, even though by his deed he makes himself unworthy of his humanity."[58] Although the immoral man is unworthy of his humanity, he has not lost that humanity, and it is precisely that humanity that grounds his dignity. Further, Kant tells us that the censure of vice "must never break out into complete contempt and denial of all moral worth to the immoral man; for on this supposition he could never be improved, and this is not consistent with the Idea of man, who as such (as a moral being) can never lose all his disposition to the good."[59]

Kant suggests that people are essentially moral beings. On his view, moral beings have moral obligations, and only autonomous beings can have moral obligations. Since dogs and frogs cannot fulfill obligations, they are not moral agents. All autonomous beings have dignity. Indeed, having autonomy grounds people's dignity. If we treat the aforementioned passages as representing Kant's view, and it seems reasonable given most everything else he says about dignity, people cannot lose their dignity, although they can certainly suffer affronts to dignity, and these can never be justified under any circumstances.

Stephen Munzer tells us that on Kant's view, unless the offending action (1) either kills the victim or (2) produces a mental disintegration that destroys the victim's capacity to act as a rational moral agent, the victim will survive as a person, "and were the victim destroyed as a person, the dignity would be destroyed rather than merely reduced."[60] I do not agree with Munzer's second condition, since Kant can get around this by saying that dignity has to do with a person's *potential* for rationality due to her humanity, or because she is the kind of thing that is capable of rationality. Munzer and I thus disagree about what Kant means by "capacity for rationality."

Kant takes dignity to be an all-or-nothing concept, or an essential property, or part of a human being's God-given essential nature—one either has it or one does not. Having dignity is like having a membership card for the "moral club," a club to which all persons belong. On this view, a person's *sense* of dignity can be reduced, but her dignity cannot. A person has a sense of dignity if she is aware of her unconditional and incomparable worth. Sense of dignity relates to self-respect.[61] A person has a proper sense of her own dignity if she has a disposition to vigorously resist being humiliated or dehumanized—but she might lack this proper sense.[62] Bernstein similarly remarks that "having self-respect reveals itself in actively valuing the self in a specific ideal under conditions of threat, say, repeated humiliations for the color of one's skin, one's language, one's religion, one's manner of dress, one's sexual orientation, one's need to work for another in order to survive."[63] On Kant's view, having dignity does not depend on having the proper sense of dignity. While a victim's sense of dignity can be lost or reduced, a victim can only lose her dignity were she destroyed as a person.

If we accept Kant's conception of dignity, we can understand the survivors' claims of harm in one of two ways. First the victims are mistaken about losing (some measure of) dignity when we use the data without their consent. Rather, their *sense* of dignity has been lost or reduced. The problem with this interpretation, however, is that it suggests that the survivors do not properly understand their harm. While this is of course possible, I argue that the survivors correctly understand their claims of harm, and so I want to find a conception of dignity that best fits their claims.

The second way to understand the survivors' claims is to assume that they are right about losing dignity when we use the data. But on Kant's account, this means that they are no longer persons, and since the survivors are not dead, they are no longer persons because they are no longer rational due to some mental degradation (presumably caused by their trauma), and so promoters of the data's use would be right in calling them emotional cripples. The problem with this interpretation is that the survivors claim that they *are* rational moral agents and the better judges in our debate. If, as I will argue, the survivors are right about being the real moral experts then they are not emotional cripples. Their emotions do not cripple their ability to know in this case.

Kant's conception of dignity does not adequately capture the survivors' claims in our debate. We must look for another conception, one suggested by survivors, as a better alternative to Kant's in explaining their claims. My proposed conception of dignity, especially its imperative to take seriously survivors' testimony and experiences, is irreconcilable with the kind of dignity that we attribute to all persons simply because they are human (that is, rational) beings. Further, it is irreconcilable with a theory that erases the victim by constructing moral meaning "solely from the perspective of the moral agent, the doer of action, forgetting the victim through the very gesture in which she is included."[64] Instead, I advocate a victim-based approach in line with Bernstein's view, a dignity driven from the perspective of victims of violence.[65] On my conception, dignity admits of degrees. In the next chapter, I first present what Holocaust survivors say about dignity, since the best account of dignity should try to incorporate what those who claim to have lost dignity say about it. Next, I consider the survivors' argument that using the data without their consent harms them. It harms their dignity or *kavod*. For this reason, we should not use the data, and even more so, survivors should have control of it to help them heal.

NOTES

1. Sandra Harding, *Whose Science? Whose Knowledge?* (Ithaca, NY: Cornell University Press, 1991), 204, my emphasis.

2. Indeed, Yehuda Bauer speaks of many Jews who refused to have their spirit broken by organizing underground social welfare, religious, cultural, and political organizations in the ghettos. See Bauer (1982, 172). In this way they were able to hold onto some of their dignity.

3. Primo Levi, "If Not Now, When? Survival in Auschwitz," in *Images from the Holocaust: A Literature Anthology*, eds. Jean Brown, et al. (Lincolnwood, IL: NTC Publishing Group, 1996), 223.

4. *Ibid.*

5. Frank Stiffel, "The Tale of the Ring: A Kaddish," in *Images from the Holocaust: A Literature Anthology*, eds. Jean Brown, et al. (Lincolnwood, IL: NTC Publishing Group, 1996).

6. Simon Wiesenthal, *The Sunflower: On the Possibilities and Limits of Forgiveness* (New York: Schocken Press, 1998), 45.

7. Joseph Kirman, "Doves on Wires," in *Truth and Lamentation: Stories and Poems on the Holocaust*, eds. Milton Teichman and Sharon Leder (Chicago: University of Illinois Press, 1994), 212.

8. Terrence Des Pres, "Excremental Assault," in *Holocaust Religious and Philosophical Implications*, eds. John Roth and Michael Berenbaum (St. Paul, MN: Paragon House, 1998).

9. Alexander Mitscherlich, *The Death Doctors*, trans. James Cleugh (London: Elek Books Ltd., 1962), 93.

10. Charles Reznikoff, *Holocaust* (Boston: Black Sparrow Press, 2007).

11. Fritz Pillwein, "Testimony at the Nuremberg Trials of War Criminals, the Medical Case, Document 912," in Alexander Mitscherlich, *The Death Doctors*, trans. James Cleugh (London: Elek Books Ltd., 1962), 113.

12. Charles Taylor, "The Politics of Recognition," in *Multiculturalism: A Critical Reader*, ed. David Theo Goldberg (Hoboken, NJ: Wiley Blackwell, 1995), 84.

13. Lawrence Langer, "The Dilemma of Choice in the Death Camps," in *Holocaust: Religious and Philosophical Implications*, eds. John Roth and Michael Berenbaum (St. Paul, MN: Paragon House, 1989), 231.

14. Friedrich Nietzsche, *The Gay Science*, Book III, Aphorism 115, trans. Josefine Nauckhoff and Adrian Del Caro (Cambridge: Cambridge University Press, 2001).

15. See "Dignity is a Useless Concept," *British Medical Journal* 327 (2003): 1419–20.

16. Immanuel Kant, *Groundwork of the Metaphysics of Morals*, trans. H. J. Paton (New York: Harper and Row, 1964), 431, 435–36.

17. Ibid., *The Doctrine of Virtue*, trans. Mary J. Gregor (New York: Harper and Row, 1964), 462–63.

18. Ibid., *Groundwork* 440, 448; *Doctrine of Virtue* 462.

19. Ibid., *Observations on the Feeling of the Beautiful and Sublime*, trans. John Goldthwait (Berkeley: University of California Press, 2004), 81.

20. Ibid., *Groundwork*, 398.

21. Stephen Munzer, "An Uneasy Case Against Property Rights in Body Parts," *Social Philosophy and Policy Foundation* (1994): 267.

22. J. M. Bernstein, *Torture and Dignity: An Essay on Moral Injury* (Chicago: University of Chicago Press, 2015), 286.

23. Christopher Stone, "Should Trees Have Standing? Toward Legal Rights for Natural Objects," in *Environmental Ethics*, ed. Louis Pojman (Belmont, CA: Wadsworth Publishing, 1998), 238.

24. Ibid., 239.

25. See Peter Singer, *Animal Liberation* (New York: Random House, 1975).

26. Kant, *Groundwork*, 438.

27. Kant uses neither "intrinsic," nor (alternatively) "inherent" value, but instead prefers the term "unconditional value," sometimes translated as "good without qualification."

28. Kant, *Groundwork*, 435.

29. Ibid., 428.

30. Ibid., 429.

31. Ibid.

32. J. M. Bernstein, *Torture and Dignity: An Essay on Moral Injury* (Chicago: University of Chicago Press, 2015), 14.

33. Onora O'Neill, "Reasons and Persons," in *Right Conduct: Theories and Applications*, ed. Michael Bayless (New York: Random House, 1983), 83.

34. Kant, *Groundwork*, 430.
35. Thomas Hobbes, *Leviathan* (Indianapolis: Hackett Publishing, 1994), 51–52.
36. Kant, *Groundwork*, 434, 436.
37. *Ibid.*, 435.
38. See Thomas Hill, *Dignity and Practical Reason in Kant's Moral Theory* (Ithaca, NY: Cornell University Press, 1992).
39. *Ibid.*, 205.
40. *Groundwork*, 433.
41. *Ibid.*
42. Sandra Harding, *Whose Science? Whose Knowledge?* (Ithaca, NY: Cornell University Press, 1991), 90–91.
43. Helen Bequaert Holmes, "Closing the Gaps: An Imperative for Feminist Bioethics," in *Embodying Bioethics: Recent Feminist Advances*, eds. Anne Donchin and Laura Purdy (Lanham, MD: Rowman & Littlefield, 1999), 54.
44. See Ronnie Janoff-Bulman, *Shattered Assumptions: Towards a New Psychology of Trauma* (New York: Free Press, 1992).
45. John D. Jones, *Poverty and the Human Condition: A Philosophical Inquiry* (New York: Edwin Mellen Press, 1990), 575.
46. Kant, *Groundwork*, 436.
47. *Ibid.*, 440.
48. Ron Bontekoe, *The Nature of Dignity* (Lanham, MD: Lexington Books, 2008), 6.
49. Kant, *Groundwork*, 436.
50. *Ibid.*, Although in Book I of *Religion Within the Limits of Reason Alone*, Kant argues that we are free even when we act contrary to the Categorical Imperative.
51. *Ibid.*, 438.
52. *Ibid.*, 434.
53. Kant, *Doctrine of Virtue*, 461–62.
54. Kant, *Groundwork*, 435.
55. *Ibid.*, 428.
56. J. M. Bernstein, *Torture and Dignity: An Essay on Moral Injury* (Chicago: University of Chicago Press, 2015), 274.
57. Sigmund Rascher, Letter dated May 15, 1941, "Document 1602 of the Nuremberg Trials of War Criminals: The Medical Case," in Alexander Mitscherlich, *The Death Doctors,* trans. James Cleugh (London: Elek Books Ltd., 1962), 24.
58. Kant, *Doctrine of Virtue*, 462.
59. Kant, *Doctrine of Virtue*, 462–63.
60. Stephen Munzer, "An Uneasy Case Against Property Rights in Body Parts," *Social Philosophy and Policy Foundation* (1994): 272.
61. *Ibid.*, 273.
62. Michael Meyer, "Dignity, Death, and Modern Virtue," *American Philosophical Quarterly* 32, no. 1 (1995): 46.
63. J. M. Bernstein, *Torture and Dignity: An Essay on Moral Injury* (Chicago: University of Chicago Press, 2015), 304.
64. *Ibid.*, 129.
65. *Ibid.*, 10.

Chapter 3

On Finding an Adequate Conception of Dignity

Lawrence Langer notes that "If we pursue the proposition that some stains of the soul of history—and the Holocaust is such a stain—are indelible, where will it lead us? It will lead us certainly . . . to the conclusion that after Auschwitz the idea of human dignity could never be the same again."[1] Not surprisingly, many survivors have described their experiences, and the lessons taken from them, in terms of dignity. Others (namely some Hebrew-speaking survivors) reject this term, preferring the word *kavod* (כָּבוֹד). But what does it mean to have *kavod*? In January 2000, at the University of Haifa, I first presented my alternative conception of dignity which I believe best captures survivor's claims of harm. Using the word "dignity" throughout my talk, I was told that when I use this term (at least in Israel), I am not speaking the same language as survivors. This was most evident when one survivor, Nathan, stood up and insisted that the appropriate word is *kavod*, not "dignity." Further, I was told that without being able to speak the language of survivors, I cannot engage in meaningful dialogue with them. This sort of problem is illustrated in the different ways that Muslims and Jews use the word "peace." According to Racel Wyman, who organizes peace negotiations between Israelis and Palestinians and whom I had the pleasure of meeting at my talk, when Muslims use the word "peace," they mean "cease fire," which is not the same as "real peace" according to Jews. Some Muslims claim that they cannot have real peace with non-Muslims. Wyman claims that when these two groups are at the table discussing "peace," much of the difficulty results from not understanding the other's use of this essential term.

"Dignity," as I found out, is not a Hebrew word. It variously translates as "human image," "honor," "respect," "importance," "nobility," and "with head held high." All are related. When Nathan insisted on *kavod* rather than "dignity," it was not that he was unfamiliar with the English term, but that he considered loss of *kavod* to be more egregious than loss of dignity. Or perhaps he was denying the existence of dignity altogether. If we take our standard conception of dignity as something that we can have on a desert island, as Kant's conception allows, then this seems right. What a great loss to be undervalued by one's community, which is what loss of *kavod* entails. Another survivor at my talk argued that dignity cannot exist without God, and God does not exist as the Holocaust attests. Here is an outright rejection of dignity.

In my talk, I stressed the importance of listening to survivors and taking their claims seriously. The audience agreed with me, and I was even cautioned to get the language right. Yet in the discussion immediately following my talk, Nathan's suggestion (that I use the word *kavod*) was callously dismissed by the academics. This exchange was a literal playing out of the debate as I had witnessed it thus far—both in the testimony of the 1989 conference and in the literature. The academics shut out the survivor and proceeded to have a discussion among themselves. To be sure, perhaps there are cultural differences between Israelis and Americans that I did not properly understand. Perhaps what I took to be a dismissal of survivors was merely the way that Israelis engage each other. Perhaps what I perceived as hostility was not hostility at all. Or perhaps it was not a difference in the way non-survivors respond to survivors, but how some academics (in this case, Israeli ones) respond to non-academics.

Nathan approached me after my talk and said that he dislikes professors because "if they specialize in the nose, they only know the right nostril." By these words, I understand Nathan to mean that academics tend to see only one side of an argument, or even stronger, that they *choose* to see only one side, thereby choosing to ignore everything else (in this case, what survivors say). Here we have Nathan attesting to epistemic arrogance. Nathan's words suggest that this was not the first time that he had experienced it. He invited me to his house for coffee, explaining "my friend Menachem and I will tell you about *kavod*!"

Kavod is essentially relational, based on societal/community recognition, approval, support, and esteem. *Kavod* is closest to "honor," "respect," even "splendor," and "majesty." It connects with one's projects. Yet Nathan told me that even Hitler had *kavod*. I told Nathan and Menachem that I require that my conception have a moral element to it, so I asked them whether there is such a thing as "good *kavod*"—something like "morally praiseworthy *kavod*." The term for this concept, I was told, is *mekhubad*, which comes from *kavod*. When I returned from my trip to Israel and met with my Hebrew professor, she told me that *mekhubad* is merely the adjectival form of *kavod*. After hearing this, I can only imagine that there was a misinterpretation or misunderstanding between Nathan, Menachem, and me. Or perhaps they meant to use *mekhubad* to signify "morally good" *kavod*. Given this possible misunderstanding, I will continue to use the word *kavod*, noting that what I have in mind is "morally good *kavod*."

Nathan and Menachem explained that one does not get *kavod* by looking for it. Rather, one gets it through "doing." Contrast this with Kantian dignity, where one need not do anything. One need only be rational. Menachem explained that one does not aim at *kavod*. The more one strives for it, the more one misses it. Rather, one gets *kavod* as a side effect of engaging in a worthy project or creating some meaningful work. However, it cannot be just any meaningful work. Rather, it must be some accomplishment that bears positively on community. If one loses *kavod*, there are many ways to gain it back. Menachem explained that he got back his *kavod* through writing about and reconstructing (in his published memoir, *The Last Way*) the eleven synagogues from his and Nathan's hometown of Brzezany, Poland (now in the Ukraine). Menachem reconstructed the dimensions of the synagogues by recalling who sat next to whom, and his dimensions were nearly perfect. He claims to have made only one mistake.

Menachem told me that all he thinks about is his town and someday rebuilding the synagogues. His life perfectly captures someone who regained, and continued to maintain, his *kavod* (for it is an ongoing process). Nathan told me that others were able to keep (at least some of) their *kavod* in the camps by engaging in works of art, preserving documents, and so on. When I went to Tel Aviv following my time in Haifa, a child of parents who were marched out of Auschwitz told me that he too understood the importance of *kavod*. His father, he explained, never regained his *kavod*.

Kavod exactly captures my alternative conception of dignity that I was trying to articulate to the Haifa audience. My conception is intersubjective, taking dignity to be a relation between people rather than a property of a person. In this way, I follow the same tradition as Ron Bontekoe and J. M. Bernstein. Bernstein, for example, argues that "the possession of dignity is neither automatic nor a metaphysical necessity, but some sort of social accomplishment."[2] Both Bontekoe and Bernstein also recognize that dignity can be destroyed. For example, Bontekoe explains that dignity is vulnerable, and those "who flatly refuse to acknowledge one's value strips one of one's dignity."[3] I do not altogether agree with Bontekoe here, for I suggest (following survivors' testimony) that one can still hold onto some measure of dignity by, for example, engaging in acts of resistance or projects of value. On my view, dignity requires (1) control in the sense of self-determination; (2) societal acknowledgment of value; (3) living a life worthy of pursuit; and (4) acting morally responsibly. At my talk at Haifa, while many people disagreed about just what term we should use when we discuss the victims' harm, my audience—and most importantly, the survivors—unanimously accepted my four conditions. Let us now consider what other survivors have said about dignity, which helps clarify my conception. Most seem to agree with survivor Jean Améry's assertion that "The mere individual, subjective claim ('I am a human being and as such I have my dignity no matter what you may do or say') is an empty academic game, or madness."[4]

Améry notes that

> I must confess that I don't know exactly what that is: human dignity. One person thinks he loses it when he finds himself in circumstances that make it impossible for him to take a daily bath. Another believes that he loses it when he must speak to an official in something other than his native language. . . . I don't know if the person who is beaten by the police loses human dignity.[5]

In all cases, the common element is a feeling of helplessness, of not having control. Dignity does not require having complete control over one's life, for no one has complete control, yet we believe that people have dignity. Rather, dignity requires having *reasonable control* over important aspects of one's life. Rousseau argues that giving up some control makes self-determination possible, and so it is necessary and rational to abandon "natural liberty" and join others in a social contract. He claims that all resultant laws are just.[6] Rousseau rightly notes that society helps make self-determination possible. The survivors, however, remind us that society is not so utopian. Some policies and treatments are not just and get in the way of self-determination.

The first of Améry's examples suggests that dignity requires control over one's body. Even stronger, as Bernstein points out, on Améry's view dignity is *rooted* in the body, rather than being external to it. Améry writes about hitting a prisoner foreman, Juszek, who struck him first without cause. Améry explains, "My human dignity lay in the punch to his jaw—and that it was in the end I, the physically much weaker man, who succumbed and was woefully thrashed, meant nothing to me. . . . My body, debilitated and crusted in filth, was my calamity. My body, when it tensed to strike back was my physical and metaphysical dignity."[7]

By hitting back, Améry demonstrated his value; he demonstrated that he possessed dignity and was not a mere *Muselmann*—a German term meaning "Muslim" (and likely originating from the similarity between the near-death prone state of a concentration camp *Muselmann* and the image of a Muslim prostrating himself on the ground in prayer), but widely used by concentration camp prisoners to refer to those inmates who were on the verge of death from starvation, exhaustion, or despair, and who had little if any chance of survival.[8] As Bernstein explains,

> The hitting back is not an act of self-defense; Améry knew, and it came to pass, that the likely outcome of striking Juszek would be an even worse thrashing

(and it could have easily provoked worse than a thrashing—his destruction). *Arousing* that worse thrashing, summoning it, is almost the point, a marker of success: it is no longer casual abuse raining down on him, but the attempt to flatten and degrade what had stood upright. Juszek's crushing—at least here—implicitly recognizes Améry's dignity (as what becomes manifest in his self-respecting action) as what is to be denied and destroyed. The stakes of hitting back are solely moral; it is about his survival as a moral being and hence as something other than a *Muselmann*.[9]

Dignity also requires control over one's mind. Lorraine Code writes about Caroline Spencer, a character in May Sarton's novel, *As We Are Now*. Sarton writes the novel in the form of a journal kept by Caroline, who is in a nursing home and given tranquilizers by her caretakers who try to "steal her mind." Caroline keeps a journal to try to maintain some sense of self and dignity. She sees herself as "an inmate in a concentration camp for the old," observing a connection between "any place where human beings are helpless, through illness or old age, and a prison."[10] Code explains that in our society we suppose old people to be, and thus treat them like, "poor things"—senile, deranged, and simple-minded—in need of tranquilizers or other treatments that turn them into "poor things."[11]

Améry's second example suggests that dignity requires control over one's environment. The disempowered, who frequently live in environments unresponsive to their needs and interests, have (often severely) limited control over their environment, and so are restricted in their life choices. Holocaust survivors, who have been robbed of control in the past, struggle in the present to maintain control over their environment. As Myra Giberovitch explains, "They may refuse help from service providers and/or their children. Some refuse to use a cane or walker or wear a hearing aid. Others are afraid to go out alone or afraid they will fall, especially during winter."[12] Améry's final example suggests that the loss of control that results in loss of dignity is of a particular type; namely, one associated with insult. Even stronger, Newton Garver explains that "to lose dignity is a violation, and (etymologically similar) *a violence*."[13]

Survivor Terrence Des Pres states that "for many among us, the word 'dignity' no longer means much . . . [if] we mean an inward resistance to determination by external forces, if we are referring to a sense of innocence and worth, something felt to be inviolate, autonomous, and untouchable, and which is most vigorous when most threatened."[14] Des Pres defines dignity as "a self-conscious, self-determining faculty whose function is to insist upon the recognition of itself as such."[15] He tells us that dignity requires control in the sense of self-determination which I suggest (as an initial definition) is the ability to choose and follow a life plan. It requires having life-plan options from which to choose. Garver explains that "if I systematically deprive a person of the options that are normal in our society, then he is no longer in a position to decide for himself what to do. Any institution, which systematically robs certain people of rightful options generally available to others, does violence to these people."[16]

As Susan Sherwin explains, choosing among unhappy alternatives when the choice is already severely limited does not constitute a "real" choice.[17] We can understand this by looking at my friend's choice of restaurant every time it is his turn to do the choosing. He knows that I am a vegetarian, and yet he insists on the local barbecue joint. He loves their beef brisket slathered in jalapeño sauce. He tells me that he does not feel badly about his choice of restaurant. After all, I can always "choose" the undressed baked potato (every other side dish—the coleslaw, the cornbread—includes bacon bits or bacon fat!).

Although I "choose" the undressed baked potato, I do not have any other real option than to choose it, if I want to stick to my vegetarian diet (and not leave hungry). I could choose to go against my vegetarian diet, but then I would be going against my moral principles. Langer refers to the Holocaust victims' "choiceless choices," in which victims often "chose" in violation of their moral principles, such as the one made by a mother who had to choose which child to save from execution in William Styron's *Sophie's Choice*. Such "choices" were deliberately and frequently forced on the camp inmates.[18]

Holocaust theologian Richard Rubenstein connects control with power and community:

> Human rights and dignity can only be attained by membership in a community that has the power to guarantee those rights. Regrettably, the word "power" must be underscored.... I do not see how one can escape the sorrowful conclusion that he alone has rights and dignity who has the power to enforce those rights or belongs to a group that possesses such power. *The possession of power is indispensable for human dignity.*[19]

According to Rubenstein, dignity is not God-given, but community-given, nor is it universal. The community decides who has dignity and who does not. Certain groups are marginalized. In those groups the members are not accorded the worth that members of more powerful groups have. Rubenstein's point is too strong, for we can think of people who have been denied power by their community, but who exercise some measure of self-determination. Consider, for example, the political prisoner who resists betraying his comrades, or the inner-city youth who refuses to allow his circumstances to control him, who refuses to "fit" his society's stereotypes of him. Such people have some measure of dignity, even though they have been denied power and are thus limited in what they can do. John Jones writes about the "dignity of the poor," of the "many poor who in the face of brutalizing conditions retain a sense of their human worth and protest against the poverty which envelops them, refusing to be beaten down by it."[20] Some survivors maintained their dignity/*kavod* in the ghettos and camps by engaging in works of art, preserving documents, and so on.

Survivor Viktor Frankl explains that "in the final analysis it becomes clear that the sort of person the prisoner becomes was the result of an inner decision and not the result of camp influences alone. Fundamentally, therefore, any man can, even under such circumstances, decide what shall become of him—mentally and spiritually. He may retain his human dignity even in a concentration camp."[21] Frankl claims that although no one chooses to endure the trauma, one can nevertheless choose how one will cope with it. As Ronnie Janoff-Bulman explains, his words remind us of William Ernest Henley's poem "Invictus" in which we are told that despite what maltreatment may come, we are the "captains of our souls."

According to Frankl, we can hold onto our dignity even in the worst of circumstances. Perhaps he is right. However, being reduced to sucking up water off of the floor, or relieving oneself of diarrhea in a soup bowl and then having to hide the bowl under one's mattress to avoid punishment or death, as camp inmates had to do, drastically affects one's sense of self-worth which in turn affects one's dignity. In being treated with less regard than one treats an animal, a person can easily accept that she is less than an animal. This leads to her accepting such dehumanizing treatment. She gives up and waits to die.

Des Pres writes that inmates were deliberately and systematically subjected to what he calls "excremental assault," a policy that aimed at the complete humiliation and debasement of the inmates.[22] Asks Des Pres, "How much self-esteem can one maintain, how readily can one respond to the needs of others, if both stink, if both are caked in mud and feces?"[23]

While Frankl is right that any person *can* hold onto her dignity in such conditions of filth and defilement, it is extremely difficult to do so. Even so, some victims retained some measure of control and dignity by caring for their appearance as an act of resistance. By insisting that any person can choose to have dignity, Frankl seems not to take into account that how we view ourselves significantly affects our reality. Janoff-Bulman tells us that people who have negative expectations of their selves and their futures (often imposed on them by societal expectations) selectively extract features of their environment that confirm these negative expectations.[24] If I expect that there is no opportunity for me to better myself then this is what I will "see," but then it is easy to accept society's low expectations of me. Jones, for example, writing about the poor on skid row, tells us that this poverty "becomes most destructive when the victims of stigmatization accept and internalize that stigmatization and come to regard themselves as worthless."[25]

Consider, for example, the stereotype of the violent, angry black male. Garver explains that when inner-city black men "lack the opportunities which they see other people, white people, around them enjoying, then they become frustrated and have great propensities to violence. The safest target for such angry, frustrated people is their own kind."[26] In acting out against other black males, the angry man fulfills society's stereotypes of him. I want to suggest that dignity is *constrained*, but not determined, by social control.

Let us now turn to one of the Judaic conceptions of dignity, since many survivors come from this tradition and so have been influenced by what it has to say. This conception of dignity is social, not metaphysical. Many survivors deny the metaphysical (God-given) conception. This social conception does not necessarily rule out the metaphysical conception. That is, one can hold both conceptions—let us call them "dignity1" and "dignity2"—perhaps even arguing that dignity2 (God-given dignity) grounds dignity1. The survivors, however, are concerned with social dignity and the role it plays in their healing, and so this will be my focus.

This conception requires autonomy, but of a different sort from Kant's. According to the *Torah umadda*, dignity is a relational concept. Rabbi Sol Roth, leader of Manhattan's Fifth Avenue Synagogue (1986–2002), explains that dignity "does not refer to a quality that is intrinsic to an individual but to a relation between the individual and the members of society in virtue of which he perceives himself and is perceived by others as deserving honor and respect."[27] Through my ongoing interactions with others, I learn about myself, and my worth, in others' eyes. A distinguishing feature of this conception of dignity is that since dignity is a relation between a person and members of a community, a person does not have dignity independent of community, just as a thing is not tall in a world in which there are no other things to which its height can be compared. Dignity is associated with height, which obviously has degrees, and originally (as with seventeenth-century philosopher Thomas Hobbes) social ranking. Dignity is associated with being able to hold one's head up in community and look others straight in the eyes.

Unlike the Kantian account, in which a person has dignity due to her humanity, dignity is a function both of a person's sense of her own self-worth and how others value her. These two are related, for a person's sense of her own self-worth is determined in large part by how others value her. This account becomes increasingly complicated when we recognize that a person can be a valued member within her own community but be disregarded by society at large. Consider Sandra Cisneros' novel, *The House on Mango Street*, in which an inner-city Latina woman must take two trains and a bus to get to the university "because she doesn't want to spend her whole life in a factory or behind a rolling pin."[28] Although her community values her, society does not encourage or may even discourage her. Although her community values her, since she knows that she belongs to a group that is not valued within society, that knowledge will affect her sense of self-worth.

If others fail to be supportive, or if they turn their backs on me, that provides me with strong evidence that I lack worth. In *Black Like Me*, John Griffin talks with an elderly black man at the Y café about the "double problem for the Negro." Explains the elderly Mr. Gayle, "First the discrimination against him. Second and almost as grievous, his discrimination against himself; his contempt for the blackness that he associates with his suffering; his willingness to sabotage his fellow Negroes because they are part of the blackness he has found so painful."[29]

On Kant's conception, having dignity does not depend on having a sense of dignity. On my account, one's sense of dignity affects how much dignity one has. If I believe that I lack self-worth, then it is easy for me to just give up (trying to improve myself, my life, and so on). But in giving up, I do not exercise what little power I might have.

The Judaic conception of dignity comes from the description of Adam in Genesis I.[30] In Genesis I, we find that God created "man" in His image. Roth explains that this image includes a person's ability to engage in creative activity.[31] He tells us that an atheist can also acknowledge the dignity of persons, not by basing that characteristic on a person's possession of the image of God, but on her uniqueness in the animal kingdom as being an animal capable of creativity and morality.

Creativity is a function of freedom. A person must be free to act "consistently and creatively on the basis of his own ideas and in a manner that accords with his commitments."[32] This is freedom in the sense of self-determination. Further, a person's creative activity must have a moral quality, since the primary characteristic of God's activities is that they are moral. One must choose and engage in a life plan worthy of pursuit.

A danger with including this criterion in my account of dignity is that we run into difficulty trying to determine just what sort of life counts as worthy of pursuit, and we face the reality that those in power often determine what counts as moral. For example, a gay man whose life plan includes raising two children with his partner was, until very recently (and still in many parts), considered to be immoral by society. We do not want just any life to be considered worthy of pursuit, however. We would want to rule out Hitler's life, for example. Lives that are destructive of one's self or others should not count as worthy lives. But even this claim is contentious. Artist Paul Gauguin quit his job and left his wife and family to pursue his artistic career, which included living a primitive life in a jungle hut in Tahiti. Some of his greatest paintings depict Tahitian life. Many would consider his life worthy despite that he left his family behind and thus denied his children a father. I do not intend to settle this issue of what counts as a worthy life, but just raise the problem as one that should be resolved.

Unlike Kant's account, in which moral responsibility follows from dignity, on my account responsibility is a condition of dignity. Hitler exerted a lot of control and power in putting to death millions of innocent people, but we would not want to say of Hitler that he had dignity. Hitler certainly acted in a dignified manner with his parades, motorcades, and grandiose speeches. His community, it seems, even acknowledged his value. But a community granting a member value is not sufficient for that member to have dignity. A community granting a member value is *necessary* for the full possession of dignity—with the denial of value comes a denial of social power, and without social power one cannot fully engage in self-determination.

Existentialist philosopher Jean Paul Sartre also grounds dignity in creativity and freedom but his account is not sufficiently social, since he claims that everyone possesses what he calls "absolute freedom," thereby ignoring social constraints on freedom. Sartre tells us that with respect to humans, "existence precedes essence." In other words, there is no universal (God-given) essence in each person. There is no pre-given meaning assigned to human existence. Since we are not given an essence, we must create one for ourselves. Each of us is "limited" to absolute freedom.[33] Despite that Sartre neglected this important social element (which was subsequently corrected by Simone De Beauvoir in her work, *The Second Sex*), his existential project—that human life must be conceived as a quest for transcendence, for flourishing and not merely preservation—is a good one to ground a notion of dignity.

Michael Meyer also connects dignity with control. He explains that one who has dignity is "self-possessed." By this he means that the person is in control of her life in at least two senses. First, she must be free from undue external coercion by others. Second, she must be free from those "all-consuming internal passions," such as those possessed by the alcoholic, the compulsive gambler, or the glutton. The person without control in these two senses lacks dignity.[34] Meyer claims that "Having dignity—*that special office or rank had by most all human beings*—is necessarily related to the possession of not only the capacity to claim rights, but at least the further capacity to exercise self-control."[35] One problem with Meyer's description is that while he rightly connects dignity with the capacity to exercise self-control (if we understand "self-control" in the sense of the ability to control one's self, broadly speaking, rather than merely controlling one's desires and temperament), he claims that most people have it, thereby ignoring the social and political character of dignity. Or perhaps he believes (I think wrongly) that for most people the social and political conditions are largely met.

A second problem is that Meyer notes that being self-possessed requires freedom from external coercion by others. Ordinarily understood, to coerce someone is to persuade or restrain that person by force, against her will with the use or threat of violence or the withholding of personal goods. When using this limited definition, perhaps Meyer is right that most people have self-control. But in using the phrase "freedom from undue external coercion," he fails to recognize the more common ways that society denies people self-control. Slaves, the "untouchables," and people living under oppressive regimes, for example, lack self-control, for they cannot even in principle better their condition. But even in the United States conditions are not much better for certain disempowered groups. In *Development as Freedom*, Amartya Sen notes that "It is remarkable that the extent of deprivation for particular groups in very rich countries can be comparable to that in the so-called Third World. For example, in the United States, African Americans as a group have no higher—indeed have a lower—chance of reaching advanced ages than do people born in immensely poorer economies."[36] And it is only getting worse. According to a 2014 *Rolling Stone* article entitled "Six Ways America Is Like a Third World Country,"

> In many American counties, especially in the deep South, life expectancy is lower than in Algeria, Nicaragua, or Bangladesh. The US is the only developed country that does not guarantee healthcare to its citizens; even after the Affordable Care Act, millions of poor Americans will remain uninsured because governors, mainly Republicans, have refused to expand Medicaid, which provides health insurance for low-income Americans.[37]

If we focus solely on infant mortality rates, we find that "there is tremendous inequality in the United States, with lower education groups, unmarried, and African American women having much higher infant mortality rates."[38] These are correlating factors. As Lindsey Cook explains in a 2015 *US News and World Report* article entitled "Why Black Americans Die Younger," "Black babies are more likely to be born to younger, less-healthy, less-wealthy and less-educated mothers, who additionally are less likely to be married and less likely to receive prenatal care than white mothers."[39]

Self-control requires the freedom to choose and pursue a life plan in a supportive community. Elisabeth Boetzkes explains that "achieving autonomy ... must be a cooperative venture, one in which the person ... benefits from having available a range of models to 'try out.'"[40] Having many life options is not sufficient, for having to choose and pursue one of several "negative, rigid, or demeaning models"[41] undermines one's self-determination and one's feeling of self-worth. For example, Audre Lorde, writing about women of color in the United States, states that "women of color ... have grown up within a symphony of anger, at being silenced, at being unchosen, at knowing that when we survive, it is in spite of a world that takes for granted our lack of humanness, and which hates our very existence outside of its service."[42]

Roth claims that "a slave has no dignity, because his conduct is invariably compelled by one whom he must serve."[43] He, like Rubenstein, does not allow the severely oppressed to have dignity. Although the seriously disadvantaged and the oppressed have severely restricted life choices, bell hooks explains that "women who are exploited and oppressed daily cannot afford to relinquish the belief that they exercise some measure of control, however relative, over their lives. They cannot afford to see themselves solely as 'victims' because their survival depends on the continued exercise of whatever personal powers they possess."[44]

Dignity, then, cannot be fully realized unless a person can exercise control, but that depends on her position of power within society. It is precisely this control that has been stolen from the Nazi victims, whose very lives (even in the most intimate details) and deaths were decided by others. According to one survivor, "When you see a lot of deaths, your mind gets numb, you cannot do nothing. . . . *Your humanity is gone.*"[45]

One question we have yet to ask in this discussion is why we value control as much as we do. Most everyone would agree that slavery, for example, is wrong, even if a person chose to sell herself into slavery and lived her life a "happy" slave. My account of dignity presupposes that freedom is one of the highest human goods. It is a fundamental good in the Rawlsian sense that no one would choose under a veil of ignorance to be a slave. But why suppose this? R. M. Hare, explaining the wrongness of slavery, tells us that when one is a slave there is always the threat of being mistreated without having the legal recourse to do anything about it. But we can build into our example that the slave has a master who has never mistreated his slaves and will never start. Further, there exists a law upheld to the highest degree stating that a slave can never be sold, and so there is no threat of mistreatment.

Hare does not allow for such "fantastic" examples. He argues that such a situation cannot occur in the "real world." Human nature, being the way that it is, people will almost always exploit those over whom they have absolute power. Since my example is not possible in the real world, I cannot use it in an argument.[46]

I do not agree with Hare. Such examples prove useful in helping us understand just what it is about slavery that we find so objectionable. Even if a person were to sell herself into "happy" slavery voluntarily, we still oppose it. Perhaps the problem consists in the person not being able to change her mind. What if sometime in the future she no longer wants to be a slave, even a happy one? Maybe the idea of life-long slavery does not bother her now, but it might later. People do enter into contracts. So what is wrong with the contract to make oneself a slave? To answer this, we should start by looking at the kind of contracts that we do not allow or that can be broken. These include those that are illegal, coerced, or those in which the person who signed the contract did so without her fully informed consent.

Let us compare (Case 1) a contract in which a person chooses to sell herself into life-long slavery to escape debt, and (Case 2) a contract in which a person from the Developing World sells her kidney to escape poverty. Currently, American drug companies collect blood in the Developing World to sell to the United States to help meet our needs. Of course the sale of organs is different, since blood is replenishable, but organs are not. Such a commercial market in organ sales has already been proposed. In such a transaction, organ brokers would get people from the Developing World to sell their organs for whatever price is needed to get them to sell. The broker would then sell those organs to Americans in need of transplantable organs. Samuel Gorovitz explains that those desperate enough to escape poverty might be willing to sell their organs, whereas under better circumstances they would not. The problem with such a contract is that "desperate circumstances can be *implicitly coercive* and the provision of excessive inducements to the oppressed can constitute a violation of their autonomy."[47]

I take "implicit coercion" to mean that such action is not outright coercive in the sense of using force or threat of force. That is, there is not a gun held to their heads, for example. Case 2 is implicitly coercive in that one would never sell one's organs except in desperate situations. Is Case 1 implicitly coercive in that one would never sell oneself into slavery except under desperate situations? In this case, the slave's life is "improved," at least insofar as she is living a debt-free existence, just as the life of the person in the Developing World is "improved" as a result of getting money for her organ. As I suggested earlier, people do things in desperate situations that they would not ordinarily do, such as my grandfather forgoing graduate school to support his widowed mother. Perhaps we see selling oneself into slavery and selling one's organs as objectionable because we strongly believe that people would never willingly do such things except under desperate circumstances—indeed, circumstances of a sort we believe should not exist.

We can show the wrongness of slavery, even if one is a happy slave, by bringing in an analogy with zoo tigers. When we think about what tigers do—pounce, chase, hunt, and so on—one of our objections to zoos is that zoo tigers cannot do what tigers do, and we think that there is something deeply wrong with that (that is, with preventing something from doing what it "naturally" does). So even if a zoo is a good zoo, we still object, since zoo tigers cannot act like wild tigers. Indeed, Holmes Rolston argues that zoo tigers are not tigers at all (but perhaps "tygers"), since an essential part of being a tiger is doing tiger-like things.[48] We find it even more tragic in the human case, since (we imagine) a zoo tiger cannot understand its situation, but a person who sells herself into slavery can.

Similarly, when we think about what people do, we include being able to make future decisions among those things. So when one sells oneself into slavery, even slavery under the very best conditions, one cannot do what people do, and there is something very wrong with that. After all, a slave cannot "undo" her choice; she cannot change her mind after she has already sold herself into slavery. Or if she does change her mind, it certainly will not make any practical difference to her circumstances. After all, she still finds herself a slave.

Roth explains that "the patient who is seriously ill and hospitalized often complains of having been robbed of dignity. This is due, not so much to the fact that he must undergo . . . embarrassing procedures, but to his helplessness and the recognition that he has lost the power to exercise control over his life."[49] Roth suggests that the patient's helplessness robs him of his dignity. A relatively recent debate, among medical ethicists and politicians, concerns whether a person has a right to die with dignity. Indeed, five states—Oregon (1994/1997), Washington (2008), Vermont (2013), California (2016), and Colorado (2016)—and the District of Columbia (2017) have Death with Dignity Laws. Advocates of such laws argue that the patient has the right to self-determination, which allows her to refuse life-sustaining treatment, or opt for the more active assisted suicide, in order to die with dignity.

While loss of dignity relates to loss of control, Améry reminds us that loss of dignity does not merely result from loss of control, but from the manner in which the control is lost. We talk about an action insulting dignity. It is loss of control in an insulting (or violent) way or being treated as not worthy of having control in the first place (Jews during the Holocaust fit the first description; the "untouchables" of India fit the second) that results in loss of dignity. The monk in a monastery who takes vows of poverty, chastity, and silence puts himself in a position in which he is extremely restricted in what he can do, but this is not insulting. Compare this to the way the inner-city person's life is restricted. Lorde speaks of women of color's anger. Anger is an appropriate response to such insult.

Is the terminally ill hospital patient losing control in an insulting way? As we have seen, an overly sensitive person can be wrong in her belief that her situation is insulting. Could a sick person be wrong about losing dignity in a hospital bed? Certain ways of dying are considered more dignified than others. In Tudor England, for example, decapitation was taken to be a dignified death whereas hanging was not, and of course most do not want to die in a brothel with one's trousers down. The assumption, in discussions about dying with dignity, is that it is insulting to be ministered to as helpless. But we should not think that being helped is necessarily insulting. That we think this (in the United States) is an unfortunate result of living in a society where autonomy is valued and dependence is scorned. Code explains that the "veneration of self-sufficiency, as a central good, produces condemnations of interdependence and collective support. . . . [People who rely] on a society's care-giving resources and systems are accorded minimal esteem."[50] While those who argue for a person's right to die with dignity correctly recognize that loss of dignity is related to control, they have the wrong conception of insult.

Changing society's conception of what counts as an insult, and understanding that the hospital patient's loss of control need not be insulting, would undermine one of the main arguments of those who advocate for assisted suicide. According to this argument, if one risks losing dignity in a hospital bed, then one should be able to die to prevent one from losing that dignity—since dignity is an important personal good. If, however, one does not lose dignity in a hospital bed (one is wrong in thinking that being helped in such ways is insulting) then the argument fails. Of course this does not rule out other reasons for supporting assisted suicide.

Can I be accused of going back to a pre-Kantian conception of dignity, since on my view dignity (or *kavod*) requires social power? Perhaps so, but this need not be negative. Dignity connects with power such that the more power one has within society, the more dignity one has. This does not mean that *all* of the powerful possess dignity. Indeed, in the case of Hitler (and we can multiply examples), having power is not sufficient. Nor does it mean that *only* the (politically, socially, economically) powerful possess dignity, for the subjugated person who exercises some measure of self-determination has some power, and so some dignity. Rather, dignity admits of degrees.

Speaking of a person having a lot of, or not much, dignity might sound strange to a Kantian. But "she has a lot of integrity" does not. We accept that people have more or less integrity (a related notion) and we have a sense of what it would take for someone to lose integrity (by betraying a loved one, for example). We must reconceive "dignity" in quantitative terms like "integrity." In his chapter entitled "Dignity in Eclipse," Bontekoe argues that non-philosophers, at least, have already moved in this direction. Among non-philosophers, "the primary meaning associated with the term 'dignity' is not that of a property universally possessed by human beings that entitles them to various forms of protection."[51] Rather, Bontekoe, citing Abraham Lincoln, claims that non-philosophers normally think that someone with dignity "bears himself under trying circumstances." In this way, dignity is "understood to be a characteristic that different people possess to different degrees."[52]

Someone might think my account offensive, since it seems that the oppressed can only achieve an "inferior version" of dignity, but since having dignity is a source of self-esteem, subjugated persons have yet one more reason to feel badly about themselves. But is dignity a source of self-esteem if everybody has it merely by belonging to the human race? For something to be a source of self-esteem, it should be earned. Kantian dignity cannot be earned. On my conception, certain aspects (our acting morally and responsibly, for example) are mostly under our control, so dignity can be a source of self-esteem after all.

Margaret Urban Walker, in a paper rejecting the view that the oppressed cannot have integrity, writes that "Terrible social burdens and injustices are born by many people with courage, dignity, and fidelity to what and whom they love."[53] She, like Frankl, holds that having dignity depends on how one responds to one's circumstances. As I understand it, "bearing injustices with dignity" is responding to one's situation in a dignified manner, or as Bontekoe puts it, bearing one's self under trying circumstances. As I have argued, acting from a *sense* of dignity contributes to having dignity. Certainly those who act this way have more dignity than those from positions of subjugation who just give up. A positive attitude prevents one from seeing oneself as lacking self-worth. If one has a negative attitude, it is easier to accept society's (real or perceived) hostility and believe that one cannot change that. Psychologists teach us that if a person expects hostility, she unwittingly behaves in ways that elicit negative behavior, just as a person who expects someone to be friendly acts in ways that bring about positive behavior.[54]

I agree with Walker that the oppressed often do "exhibit valor, perseverance, lucidity, and ingenuity in staying true to what they value within the confines of their situation."[55] On my view, such people have some measure of dignity, and in many cases have more dignity than those with more power since it does not follow (and history has demonstrated) that just because one is more powerful, one acts morally or responsibly.

Someone might object that without Kantian dignity, one would have no grounds on which to demand respectable treatment. This is like pulling out one's "dignity card" before the first punch and asserting, "You cannot hurt me, because I am one of you." If a person refuses to treat another well, pleas of dignity will not help. Further, being human should be enough for respectable treatment, or being a creature capable of suffering, or being alive. Why should we make a further appeal to the moral equivalent of phlogiston? But if someone has less dignity, this does not give others the right to treat her like a thing or deprive her of the status of person.[56] Instead, we should work toward that person's flourishing. Similarly, one might argue that without (God-given) dignity people have no value. But we can speak of someone having value without ever appealing to this metaphysical conception of dignity—in terms of her capacity to suffer, reason, make moral decisions, create, and so on. Further, my conception of dignity does not rule out a person having sanctity.

As Holocaust survivors so vividly tell us, having dignity directly relates to having control, and we cannot deny that people possess varying degrees of control. Not everyone is equally positioned within society. Many people are disadvantaged, exploited, depend on the care of others, or are responsible for the care of others, and so are limited in what they can do. On my account, how much control one has really affects one's worth, and not merely one's sense of worth. Here, society in large part determines one's worth, and so my account is, in this sense, Hobbesian. Kant's account assumes that all people are treated alike in a kingdom of ends. His account does not recognize difference. By contrast, my account is not idealistic. Having dignity does not mean having (God-given) worth in virtue of being a rational, autonomous agent. Having dignity means having the power to engage in one's meaningful projects, and with that power comes responsibility.

Since Judaism is a "this worldly" rather than "other worldly" religion, its primary concern is with the character of community and our responsibilities within it. As Roth notes, were it primarily other worldly, it would be concerned with preparing people to achieve the "ultimate spiritual goal" interpreted in other worldly terms.[57] Being this worldly, Judaism recognizes that we must work to improve the situations of people of color, the poor, residents of the Developing World, victims of unethical medical research (who tend to be the disadvantaged and already exploited), and other disenfranchised persons.

My conception of dignity can be enriched by a discussion of the less well known—at least to many Western readers—Hindu conception of dignity. According to Hinduism, there are ten human virtues: love, trust, compassion, truthfulness, righteousness, tolerance, beneficence, sacrifice, forgiveness, and rationality. These virtues constitute human dignity and are mostly distinct to human beings. Recognition of these virtues constitutes respect. Respect, then, is recognition of dignity. While I would not say that such virtues *constitute* human dignity, many seem necessary to fulfilling dignity's four conditions.

We can clearly see how some of these virtues can be stolen from a person in human-inflicted trauma, and especially a trauma like the Holocaust. Loss of beneficence, love, trust, compassion, and rationality can be seen in, for example, the following passage from Elie Wiesel's *Night* where a son kills his father for a piece of bread: "Felled to the ground, stunned with blows, the old man cried: 'Meir. Meir my boy! Don't you recognize me? I'm your father . . . you're hurting me . . . you're killing your father! I've got some bread . . . for you too . . . for you too.'"[58]

Restoring love and trust requires time, cooperation with community, and perhaps a public reconciliatory effort such as, in our case, doing what survivors say with respect to the data. Forgiveness may be more difficult, and I suggest neither morally required nor expected in the case of the Holocaust and other atrocities. That is, if some acts should not be forgiven, human atrocity like the Holocaust would certainly count if anything does. A close look at these ten virtues also helps us see the interdependence of dignity, for restoring survivors' love and trust, for example, requires community members' compassion, tolerance, and perhaps even sacrifice. This suggests that community members lack full dignity when they fail to exercise those virtues necessary for the survivors' healing.

The conception of dignity that I offer might not sit well with people. It offends the ears to hear that some people have it and others do not, and that some people have more dignity than others. But with this statement comes an injunction to make the community a better place by giving people control and the responsibility to exercise that control. Having laid out my account of dignity, I must next show (1) how trauma affects the self; (2) what is required to heal from trauma; and (3) how in our case this requires controlling the data. I do this in the next chapter.

NOTES

1. Lawrence Langer, "The Dilemma of Choice in the Death Camps," in *Holocaust: Religious and Philosophical Implications*, eds. John Roth and Michael Berenbaum (St. Paul, MN: Paragon House, 1989), 231.
2. J. M. Bernstein, *Torture and Dignity: An Essay on Moral Injury* (Chicago: University of Chicago Press, 2015), 280.
3. Ron Bontekoe, *The Nature of Dignity* (Lanham, MD: Lexington Books, 2008), 105.
4. Jean Améry, quoted in *Approaches to Auschwitz: The Holocaust and its Legacy*, eds. Richard Rubenstein and John K. Roth (Louisville, KY: Westminster John Knox Press, 2003), 374.
5. Jean Améry, "Torture," in *Holocaust Religious and Philosophical Implications*, eds. John Roth and Michael Berenbaum (St. Paul, MN: Paragon House, 1989), 177.
6. See Jean-Jacques Rousseau, *The Social Contract and Other Later Political Writings*, trans. Victor Gourevitch (Cambridge: Cambridge University Press, 1997).
7. Jean Améry, *At the Mind's Limit: Contemplations by a Survivor on Auschwitz and Its Realities* (Bloomington: Indiana University Press, 2009), 90–91.
8. See "Muselmann," at yadvashem.org.
9. J. M. Bernstein, *Torture and Dignity: An Essay on Moral Injury* (Chicago: University of Chicago Press, 2015), 308, emphasis in the original.
10. May Sarton, *As We Are Now*, quoted in Lorraine Code, *Rhetorical Spaces: Essays on Gendered Location* (New York: Routledge, 1995), 84.
11. Lorraine Code, *Rhetorical Spaces: Essays on Gendered Location* (New York: Routledge, 1995), 86.
12. Myra Giberovitch, *Recovering from Genocidal Trauma: An Information and Practice Guide for Working with Holocaust Survivors* (Toronto: University of Toronto Press, 2014), 108.
13. Newton Garver, *What Violence Is*," in *Social Ethics*, eds. Thomas Mappes and James Zembaty (New York: McGraw-Hill, 1977), 274, my emphasis.
14. Terrence Des Pres, "Excremental Assault," in *Holocaust Religious and Philosophical Implications*, eds. John Roth and Michael Berenbaum (St. Paul, MN: Paragon House, 1989), 213.

15. *Ibid.*

16. Newton Garver, "What Violence Is," in *Social Ethics*, eds. Thomas Mappes and James Zembaty (New York: McGraw-Hill, 1977), 274.

17. Susan Sherwin, "Feminism and Bioethics," in *Feminism and Bioethics, Beyond Reproduction*, ed. Susan Wolf (Oxford: Oxford University Press, 1996), 58.

18. Lawrence Langer, "The Dilemma of Choice in the Death Camps," in *Holocaust: Religious and Philosophical Implications*, eds. John Roth and Michael Berenbaum (St. Paul, MN: Paragon House, 1989), 230.

19. Richard Rubenstein, "An Exchange," in *Holocaust: Religious and Philosophical Implications*, eds. John Roth and Michael Berenbaum (St. Paul, MN: Paragon House, 1989), 359, my emphasis.

20. John D. Jones, *Poverty and the Human Condition: A Philosophical Inquiry* (New York: Edwin Mellen Press, 1990), 562.

21. Viktor Frankl, *Man's Search for Meaning*, quoted in Ronnie Janoff-Bulman *Shattered Assumptions: Towards a New Psychology of Trauma* (New York: Free Press, 1992), 135.

22. Terrence Des Pres, "Excremental Assault," in *Holocaust Religious and Philosophical Implications*, eds. John Roth and Michael Berenbaum (St. Paul, MN: Paragon House, 1989), 209.

23. *Ibid.*, 210.

24. Ronnie Janoff-Bulman, *Shattered Assumptions: Towards a New Psychology of Trauma* (New York: Free Press, 1992), 32.

25. John D. Jones, *Poverty and the Human Condition: A Philosophical Inquiry* (New York: Edwin Mellen Press, 1990), 562.

26. Newton Garver, "What Violence Is," in *Social Ethics*, eds. Thomas Mappes and James Zembaty (New York: McGraw-Hill, 1977), 274.

27. Sol Roth, *The Jewish Idea of Culture* (Hoboken, NJ: KTAV Publishing House, 1997), 69.

28. Sandra Cisneros, *The House on Mango Street* (New York: Vintage Books, 1984), 32.

29. John Griffin, *Black Like Me* (New York: Signet Books, 1996), 45.

30. This is the conception of dignity as given in the *Torah umadda*. The *Torah im derech eretz* gives an alternative account of dignity. On this view, a person possesses dignity in virtue of acting as God's representative on earth.

31. Sol Roth, *The Jewish Idea of Culture* (Hoboken, NJ: KTAV Publishing House, 1997), 70.

32. *Ibid.*

33. Jean Paul Sartre, *Being and Nothingness*, in John Iuculano and Keith Burkum, "The Humanism of Sartre: Toward a Psychology of Dignity," *Journal of Theoretical and Philosophical Psychology* 16, no. 1 (1996): 23.

34. See Michael Meyer, "Dignity, Rights, and Self Control," *Ethics* (1989), and "Dignity, Death, and Modern Virtue," *American Philosophical Quarterly* 32, no. 1 (1995).

35. Michael Meyer, "Dignity, Rights, and Self Control," *Ethics* (1989): 533, my emphasis.

36. Amartya Sen, *Development as Freedom* (New York: Random House, 2000), 21.

37. Sean McElwee, "Six Ways America is Like a Third World Country," *Rolling Stone*, March 5, 2014.

38. Christopher Ingraham, "Our Infant Mortality Rate is a National Embarrassment," *Washington Post*, September 29, 2014.

39. Lindsey Cook, "Why Black Americans Die Younger," *US News and World Report*, January 5, 2015.

40. Elizabeth Boetzkes, "Equality, Autonomy, and Feminist Bioethics," in *Embodying Bioethics: Recent Feminist Advances*, eds. Anne Donchin and Laura Purdy (Lanham, MD: Roman & Littlefield, 1999), 123.

41. *Ibid.*

42. Audre Lorde, "The Uses of Anger: Women Responding to Racism," in *Sister Outsider* (Trumansburg, NY: The Crossing Press, 1984), 129.

43. Sol Roth, *The Jewish Idea of Culture* (Hoboken, NJ: KTAV Publishing House, 1997), 70.

44. bell hooks, *Feminist Theory: From Margin to Center* (Boston: South End Press, 1984), 45.

45. Lawrence Langer, *Holocaust Testimonies: The Ruins of Memory* (New Haven, CT: Yale University Press, 1993), 84, my emphasis.

46. See R. M. Hare, "What is Wrong with Slavery?" in *Applied Ethics*, ed. Peter Singer (Oxford: Oxford University Press, 1986).

47. Samuel Gorovitz, "Procurement and Allocation of Human Organs for Transplantation," *Hearings Before the Subcommittee on Investigations and Oversight of the Committee on Science and Technology*, Ninety-Eighth Congress, First Session, No. 71 (1983), 77, my emphasis.

48. See Holmes Rolston, *Environmental Ethics: Duties to and Values in the Natural World* (Philadelphia: Temple University Press, 1988).

49. Sol Roth, *The Jewish Idea of Culture* (Hoboken, NJ: KTAV Publishing House, 1997), 70.

50. Lorraine Code, *Rhetorical Spaces: Essays on Gendered Location* (New York: Routledge, 1995), 108.

51. Ron Bontekoe, *The Nature of Dignity* (Lanham, MD: Lexington Books, 2008), 1.

52. *Ibid.*

53. Margaret Urban Walker, "Picking Up Pieces," in *Feminists Rethink the Self*, ed. Diana Tietjens Meyer (Boulder, CO: Westview Press, 1997), 76.

54. Ronnie Janoff-Bulman, *Shattered Assumptions: Towards a New Psychology of Trauma* (New York: Free Press, 1992), 32–33.

55. Margaret Urban Walker, "Picking Up Pieces," in *Feminists Rethink the Self*, ed. Diana Tietjens Meyer (Boulder, CO: Westview Press, 1997), 76.

56. Michael Meyer, "Dignity, Rights, and Self Control," *Ethics* (1989): 529.

57. Sol Roth, *The Jewish Idea of Culture* (Hoboken, NJ: KTAV Publishing House, 1997), 125.

58. Elie Wiesel, *Night*, trans. Stella Rodway (New York: Avon, 1969), 96.

Chapter 4

Trauma, the Self, and Controlling the Nazi Data

Philosopher Charles Taylor writes that having a self requires being "oriented in moral space, a space in which questions arise about what is good or bad, what is worth doing and what is not, what has meaning and importance for you and what is trivial and secondary."[1] Lawrence Langer accuses Taylor of "insularity" and "innocence," of using a definition suitable only for a society in which people are free to make choices.[2] The Holocaust victims were not part of such a society. I have now reached the next steps of my argument presented at the beginning of chapter 2. I must (1) explain how trauma affects the self (rendering the victim out of control) and how recovery from trauma requires regaining control; (2) show how the survivors' recovery specifically requires controlling the data; and (3) describe how the survivors' dignity can be restored posthumously, in the continuation of their projects. Let us begin with two survivors' accounts.

In his poem, "Draft of a Reparations Agreement," Holocaust survivor Dan Pagis responds to *Wiedergutmachung*, the German government's postwar promise to "making good again," wryly assuring that everything will return to their places. "The scream back into the throat./The gold teeth back to the gums./The terror."[3] Another survivor David Rousset writes, "Normal men do not know that everything is possible. . . . The concentrationees do know. . . . *For years on end they groped their way through the fantastic scenes littered with the ruins of human dignities. . . .*"[4] Rousset calls the survivors "living corpses" condemned to a life of "vain convalescence."

Pioneer psychologist of trauma, Judith Herman, explains that human-inflicted trauma violates the autonomy of the person at the level of basic bodily integrity. The body is invaded, injured, and defiled.[5] Even after the trauma, survivors often cannot attend to basic health needs or bodily functions such as sleeping, eating, and in the Holocaust survivors' case, even urinating and defecating. Cynthia Lancaster et al., writing about post-traumatic stress disorder (PTSD) in trauma survivors, further note that many survivors experience recurrent intrusive memories, traumatic nightmares, and flashbacks, engage in avoidance behavior, and experience hypervigilance, sleep disturbance, and difficulty concentrating.[6]

Trauma also results in the survivor losing control over his environment. One survivor explains to an interviewer his utter helplessness at the moment the Nazis took him, his wife, and their infant child:

> This was summer. Outside there was a bench. So we sat on the bench. . . . In my head, what to think of first. You want to do something and you know you're in a corner. You can't do anything. And when somebody asks me now "Why didn't you fight?" [voice breaking, tears, a tone and look of utter despair at the moment remembered] I ask them "How would you fight in such a situation?"[7]

The victim no longer lives in safety. He can no longer provide a safe environment for his family. He is forced to stand by, helplessly watching violence committed against the people he loves most. Losing control over one's environment also includes losing mobility and a plan for self-protection.[8] As the survivor above attests, the victim finds himself cornered. Commonly a rape survivor cannot bring herself to walk outside, her fear literally prevents her from doing so. This drastically affects the survivor's self.

Consider the following testimony:

I didn't know who I was; I had doubts about my own name. I remembered only my prison number, as if it were engraved on my brain.[9]

I wasn't even alive; I wasn't even alive. . . . But yet I survived.[10]

Sometimes I wonder whether the person inside me who was a child during the war comes from the same root as I, has lived the same experiences, has seen what I have seen.[11]

Herman tells us that trauma "shatters the construction of the self that is formed and sustained in relation to others."[12] Trauma destroys the survivor's relationships with family, friends, and community. As philosopher Laurence Thomas explains,

> Immediately following the tragedy of rape, a victim—say, Naomi—may feel especially uncomfortable with being supportively hugged or, for that matter, merely supportively touched by her close male friends—say, Richard and James—though the three of them have been longstanding friends for years and there have been many physical (but nonsexual) displays of affection between her and them.[13]

We develop a secure sense of connection with caring people early in childhood. Such a connection serves as the basis for personality development. Trauma severs this connection and the survivor loses her basic sense of self. The traumatic event reawakens developmental struggles (with autonomy, competence, identity, and intimacy) resolved in childhood and adolescence. Thomas explains that children are born without a sense of personal agency, but acquire it under favorable situations with adult caretakers who teach them appropriate care of their bodies. Infants begin life with bodily care being routinely performed on their behalf by adults. As the child gets older, she performs routine bodily care under the watchful eyes of her caretakers, who offer occasional assistance. If all goes well, the adolescent is left to care for her own body. As Thomas aptly puts it, "The fourteen-year-old is told to take a shower, not given one."[14]

Caretakers who give their child complete control over bodily care help establish and reinforce the child's sense of personal agency. The child learns that she has boundaries and she trusts others to respect those boundaries. A traumatic event, such as rape, destroys that trust, leaving the victim vulnerable and shaking her "sense of personal agency at its very core, regardless of how well-developed that sense might be."[15] How much worse it is for the child victim who has yet to develop a secure sense of self.

Many trauma survivors lose trust in their selves, in other people, and (if they were believers) even in God. Feelings of helplessness, humiliation, and guilt assault their belief in their own self-worth. Lancaster et al. note that survivors often have distorted beliefs about their selves and the world, persistent shame or guilt, emotional numbing, and feelings of alienation.[16] Rachel Yehuda similarly explains that "horror, anger, sadness, humiliation, and guilt can also occur in response to trauma."[17] Herman tells us that there exists "a direct relationship between the severity of the trauma and its psychological impact, whether the impact is measured in terms of the number of people affected or the intensity and duration of harm."[18] While Naomi, in Thomas' example, will no doubt eventually take comfort in and enjoy the company of her friends Richard and James, the Holocaust survivor has much more difficulty in her future relations with others. Gerda, a character in E. M. Broner's novel, *A Weave of Women*, lost her family to the Nazis. She tells her female companions that as a result of her experiences she can do just about everything with her body:

> My body can walk miles. My feet never get bunions, calluses, or plantar warts.... My hands are not afraid of stings, pressings of the pencil, of holding test tubes delicately, of being burned or cut.... I go on the March to Jerusalem, and I alone could still circle the city another three times.... I have climbed Mount Sinai without losing breath, four hours each way. I came down hungry and ready to cook a meal for a crowd.[19]

But when asked what her body cannot do, Gerda replies after a long silence, "It doesn't know how to feel what other people are feeling. Since the camps, I have been careful not to know too much about my surroundings."[20] She begins to cry.

Herman explains that prolonged captivity, such as that experienced in a concentration camp, produces profound alterations in the victim's identity. All of the psychological structures of the self "have been invaded and systematically broken down. . . . Even after release from captivity, *the victim cannot assume her former identity*."[21] Her new identity must include memories of her enslaved self. Rachel Brenner explains that "life after the Holocaust has not attenuated the past of horror; the ongoing struggle with the memories in the post-Holocaust 'normal' world has become, in fact, the continuation of the struggle for survival that took place 'over there.'"[22]

Many trauma survivors lose the sense that they have a self at all. In her paper "Outliving Oneself: Trauma, Memory, and Personal Identity," philosopher and rape survivor Susan Brison writes that human-inflicted trauma is "self-annihilating." Therapists who help Holocaust survivors often hear this. While the majority of their patients claim, "I am now a different person," the most severely traumatized state, "I am not a person." For example, survivor Charlotte Delbo writes that "I died in Auschwitz, but no one knows it."[23]

Recall that Taylor requires that the self be oriented in "moral space" in which questions arise about what is (1) good and bad; (2) worth doing and not; and (3) meaningful and important. Langer criticizes Taylor for defining the self in terms that effectively exclude people who are in places like Auschwitz. Yet some survivors claim that the concentration camp left them without a self, and so they would agree with Taylor. But in saying this, they do not mean to suggest that they therefore cannot now make judgments about themselves or the community. Many make such judgments and want others to take them seriously. Indeed, many claim to be moral experts in our debate, by virtue of their experiences, a claim that we will revisit later in this work.

I have discussed how trauma renders the victim out of control and how trauma drastically alters the victim's self. The most damaging effect of trauma is the loss of one's moral self (or perhaps better, the victim finds herself having to *reconstruct* her moral self, since the rules by which she learned her morality no longer exist, and so she is left with having to create a *new* moral self without the tools to accomplish this.) In distinguishing between "self" and "moral self" I do not want to suggest that people have two selves, or that what we call the "self" is not fundamentally moral. I make this distinction to highlight the ways in which trauma affects different aspects of the self.

Survivor George S. writes, "I was ashamed of the whole thing—it was so shameful. It was so degrading. . . . Families were beginning to—some were even fighting among themselves over a piece of bread. Some were stealing from each other. It was horrible. Some became informers to the Germans for a piece of bread."[24] As Herman explains, the perpetrator completes his psychological control of the victim when he forces her to violate her own moral principles. "Psychologically, this is the most destructive of all coercive techniques, for the victim who has succumbed loathes herself."[25] Psychologists of trauma note that women of domestic violence, for example, often violate their moral principles by (1) being forced to engage in sexual practices that they find immoral or disgusting; (2) being forced to cover up their partner's actions; (3) being pressured to participate in illegal activities; and (4) "sacrificing" their children who are themselves often victims of physical or sexual abuse. In *The Second Sex*, Simone De Beauvoir, describing a woman's situation, similarly writes, "She knows that masculine morality, as it concerns her, is a vast hoax. Man pompously thunders forth his code of virtue and honor, but in secret, he invites her to disobey it, and he even counts on this disobedience."[26]

Herman describes two stages in the psychological breakdown of the concentration camp victim. In the first stage, the victim "relinquishes her inner autonomy, world view, moral principles, or connection with others for the sake of survival. . . . There is a shutting down of feelings, thoughts, initiative, and judgment."[27] The first stage is reversible. In the second stage, the victim reaches a state of absolute passivity. She loses the will to live. Survivor Tadeusz Borowski writes about the "Muslims" (also called *Muselmanner*), the camp name for inmates destroyed physically and spiritually and who lack the strength and will to go on living—people, he claims, who are "ripe" for the gas chamber.[28] Yehuda Bauer calls such people little more than "walking automatons." In her *Origins of Totalitarianism,* Hannah Arendt refers to the Nazis' "institutionalized humiliation" which resulted in the "insane mass manufacture of corpses . . . preceded by the historically and politically intelligible preparation of *living corpses.*"[29] J. M. Bernstein also recognizes that "the exorbitance of Nazi practice was that it turned the legislative *denial* of dignity into the practical *destruction* of dignity—ending with mass, *anonymous* death.[30]

The victims' loss of moral self is built into the concentration camp experience. Langer explains that "when the environment in Auschwitz supported one person's life, it was often at the cost of another's death—not because victims made wrong choices, or no choices, but because dying was the 'purpose' of living in this particular environment."[31] The victims entered the concentration camps with the belief that they had control over what they did, that they could make moral choices, and so on. The camp environment, one of "choiceless choice," shattered these assumptions. For example, women "chose" to suffocate or drown their babies to prevent themselves from being discovered and killed. Further, the Nazis had a law stating that any mother who refused to surrender her newborn to the gas chamber was sent to death with her child, forcing the mother to "choose" her child's death for her own survival. Langer speaks of the victims being profoundly disturbed by this loss of moral dimension in their lives.

In his work, *This Way for the Gas, Ladies and Gentleman*, Borowski writes about the "Canadians," the camp name for the special detachment force of inmates who helped unload incoming transports of people destined for the gas chambers. The narrator's friend, Henri, invites him to join him for ramp duty, promising his choice of clothes. "'Don't take any money,' Henri warns his friend, 'they might be checking. Anyway, who the hell needs money? . . . Don't take suits, either, or they'll think you're planning to escape. Just get a shirt, silk only, with a collar. And a vest.'"[32]

The Canadians would unload people and luggage off of the cattle cars. They would force them to remove all of their clothing and valuables and then shove them into trucks (packed sixty to a truck, like sardines) headed for the gas chambers. Canadians were so called for their amassing great wealth by taking valuables from the people headed for death. They would steal clothing, vodka, and perfume for themselves, and they were fed well. It is curious that they were called "Canadians" rather than "Americans," since Americans, and not Canadians, are stereotypically exploitative of others. Many Canadians committed suicide because they found themselves so morally disgusting.

Wiesel writes about watching his father being beaten while he stood by and did nothing:

> I had watched the whole scene without moving. I kept quiet. In fact, I was thinking of how to get farther away so that I would not be hit myself. What is more, any anger I felt at that moment was directed, not at the [guard], but against my father. I was angry with him, for not knowing how to avoid Idek's outbreak. That is what concentration camp life had made of me.[33]

Pierre, a survivor of Mauthausen, talks about his encounter with an inmate suffering from a facial phlegmon. The pain caused the man to moan constantly. "Finally one night in the barracks, three inmates unable to sleep because of the noise carried the man to a separate bunk, held his legs and suffocated him to death with a pillow." Pierre stood by and watched his fellow inmates kill the man. He asks despairingly, "What could I say? What could you do? Nothing! Nothing!"[34]

Survivor Calel Perechodnik became a ghetto policeman. He explains, "Seeing that the war was not coming to an end and in order to be free from the roundup for labor camps, I entered the ranks of the Ghetto Polizei."[35] His duties included assisting the Nazis in roundup and deportation of Jews to the gas chambers at Treblinka. Among those deported were his wife and child.

His memoir is entitled *Am I a Murderer?* to which Perechodnik answers "yes."

Not every camp inmate lost his moral self. Claudia Card, writing about Simon Wiesenthal, explains, "It never seems to occur to [Wiesenthal] to take anything but a moral approach to question after question about what to do and whether his choices were the right ones. He did not find oppression an excuse, or even an occasion, for moral insensitivity."[36] We need to be careful about what Card's subtext suggests. It would be inappropriate, for example, to blame those many victims who did succumb to what those of us in the "normal" world would call immoral acts. In his work, *Moral Responsibility in the Holocaust*, David Jones explains that "people who intentionally do something wrong sometimes act from motives that do not reflect badly on their character, or if they do, they bring only slight discredit on them because their motives and relative lack of control are understandable in the situation."[37] As we have seen, the camp experience forced people to act in ways most would never ordinarily act. John Roth explains how the Nazis "capitalized on a cunning that enticed and then required Jews to participate in the annihilation of their own people."[38] In so doing, the Nazis destroyed the inmates' fundamental assumptions about the world.

Another pioneer in the psychology of trauma, Ronnie Janoff-Bulman, claims that most of us hold fundamental assumptions about the world. These include: (1) that the world is benevolent; (2) that the world is meaningful; (3) that the self is worthy; and (4) that we can directly control what happens to us through our own behavior.[39] These beliefs originate in our earliest experiences with our caretakers, usually our mothers. The infant generalizes about the goodness of the world and herself within it by observing that "there is someone good who cares about me and I can do certain things to bring about a caring response. Therefore, I must be worthy of care."[40]

As Janoff-Bulman explains, during their prolonged period of dependency, children who are loved and well cared for develop a deeply rooted sense of safety, security, and their own invulnerability. As a result, we generally underestimate the likelihood of negative outcomes, and even when we do recognize the possibility of bad things happening, we believe ourselves to be more or less invulnerable. The world is not random. We can control what happens to us through our own behavior. Bad things only happen to bad or careless people. Psychologists call this belief the "just world hypothesis." It is comforting to believe that we can control outcomes, that what we do makes a difference.

Janoff-Bulman tells us that we often hold onto these beliefs about the benevolence of the world and our ability to control what happens to us in it, even in the face of contradictory evidence. Changes in these beliefs are likely to occur, if they occur at all, gradually rather than suddenly. This helps us understand why the majority of Jews were unwilling to believe what was happening to them. As Bauer explains, annihilation was inconceivable to them: "Thousands of Jews died disbelieving what was going on before their very eyes."[41]

The first and major obstacle was accepting an "impossible reality—a contradiction in terms." Wiesel, after witnessing infants and children being burned alive in a pit of flames, expressed his disbelief in such a reality to his father: "I told [my father] that I did not believe that they could burn people in our age, that humanity could never tolerate it." His father answered, "Humanity? Humanity is not concerned with us. Today anything is allowed. Anything is possible, even these crematories."[42]

The narrator of Jorge Semprun's novel *What a Beautiful Sunday* writes, "There is no such thing as innocent memory. Not for me anymore."[43] In the immediate aftermath of traumatic events, victims experience the terror of their own vulnerability. Yehuda notes that experiencing a traumatic event "challenges a person's sense of safety, leading to feelings of vulnerability and powerlessness."[44] Janoff-Bulman explains that the victim asks "why me?" and finds herself unable to fit the traumatic experience with her long-standing, comfortable beliefs about herself and the world. She tries desperately to reconcile her trauma with her beliefs that the world is benevolent, she has control over negative outcomes, and she is immune from bad things happening because she is a good and attentive person. The survivor's inner world becomes pervaded by "thoughts and images representing malevolence, meaninglessness, and self-abasement."[45] Given these debilitating effects of trauma, how does the survivor recover from it?

Survivor Isabella Leitner writes,

> From time to time it dawns on us that we have been detached from the rest of humankind. We will have to relearn how to live, how to hold a fork, how to live with the family of man. Too great a task. The resources within us will have to stand up to a nearly impossible struggle. . . . We know almost everything about life and death. Still, we have to relearn how to walk step by painfully fragile step.[46]

Leitner discusses the enormous difficulty in regaining control and reconnecting with ordinary life. Tasks that non-victims take for granted, such as caring for themselves or relating to others, seem "too great." Yet as Herman recognizes, since trauma robs the victim of power and control, "the guiding principle of recovery is to restore power and control to the survivor."[47]

The survivor's central and immediate concern is to regain control over her body (which includes managing post-traumatic symptoms) and reestablish a safe environment in which she can reengage in ordinary tasks. As the survivor continues to heal, she begins to engage more actively in the world and reconnect with others. Herman explains that by the final stage of recovery, the survivor recognizes that she has been a victim and understands the effects of her victimization. *Now she is ready to protect herself and others against future danger.* Reconnecting with others brings the survivor in contact with the next generation. As Herman puts it, "Concern for the next generation is *always linked to the question of prevention.* The survivor's overriding fear is a repetition of the trauma. Her goal is to prevent a repetition at all costs. 'Never again!' is the survivor's universal cry."[48]

Consider the following poetry by survivors, their witnesses, and their advocates, which speaks to feelings of self-blame and guilt:

I who lay between the mountain of myrrh
and the hill of frankincense,
dead and surviving, and dared not breathe,
and asked, By what right am I myself?
Who I am I do not know,
but I believe myself to be one
who should have died, and the dead one
who did die. . . .[49]

The sun rose over a mound of corpses
And one, who witnessed it, asked:
—Are you not ashamed to rise, sun?
He asked and received no reply,
For in that moment he said to himself:
—Are you not ashamed to live on?
And he sat down opposite the mount,
And looked at the bodies as they lay,
. . .And in that moment he said to himself:
—Are you not ashamed to sit while they lie—
And he lay down, like one of the dead,
Face up, and lay this way for hours.
While he lay there, a melody rose within him
That sang of his own shame,
. . .And the mount of corpses
Picked up his melody
And answered with an echo
Like a resounding choir.[50]

Bertolt Brecht writes that he knows that it's simply luck that he survived, "But last night in a dream/I heard those friends say to me: 'Survival of the fittest'/And I hated myself."[51]

Yehuda explains that many survivors "blame themselves for failing to act in ways that could have averted the event or mitigated the circumstances of the event."[52] Such practices help them regain control and thus restore their belief in a controllable world. If the survivor can convince herself that she is to blame for her victimization—or as is most often the case with Holocaust survivors, *for her survival*—she can maintain her belief in a controllable world. This works to maximize the survivor's feelings of control (thereby reestablishing some sense of invulnerability) and minimize feelings of helplessness.

The survivor who reinterprets the traumatic event as one in which she is to blame for either her trauma or her survival often (obsessively) engages in new behaviors to protect herself and others against future atrocities, believing that she can (and indeed must) make a difference. As Janoff-Bulman explains, "To believe one can make a difference is very comforting. This is the belief structure of non-victims who assume they are relatively invulnerable."[53] Such strategies should diminish over time as the survivor integrates the trauma into her previous world. The survivor's belief that she *must* prevent future atrocities should also diminish over time. However, those who were most severely traumatized often get stuck at this stage of self-blame, guilt, and obsession. Langer describes the Holocaust survivors' experiences as a "festering wound" rather than a "scar." A scar, unlike a wound, suggests a past injury, healed in the present. It should come as little surprise then that these survivors still blame themselves and feel intensely guilty for surviving while so many others lost their lives, as the following testimony attests: "I told my little kid brother, I said to him, 'Solly, gey tsu Tate un Mame [go to poppa and momma].' And like a little kid, he followed—he did. Little did I know that I sent him to the crematorium. I am . . . I feel like I killed him."[54] As Langer explains, the survivor would rather blame himself for his brother's death than "embrace the law of systematic caprice that governed the selection process."[55] The latter suggests an unacceptable randomness and malevolence to the world. Survivor William R. explains how he desperately tried, but failed, to save his brother from the gas chambers. He writes,

> I'll never forgive myself. Even if I want it, I can't. . . . When I came to the gate where the selection was, then the Gestapo said to me (I showed him my papers), "You go to the right." I said, "This is my brother." He whipped me over the head, he said, "He goes to the left." And from this time I didn't see any more my brother. . . . I have nightmares, and I think all the time, that the young man, maybe he wouldn't go with me, maybe he would survive. It's a terrible thing.

It's almost forty years and it's still bothering me. I still got my brother on my conscience. God forgive me![56]

The concentration camp experience was especially conducive to self-blame, leaving it easy for the survivor to adopt (and maintain) this adaptive strategy once she returned to the "normal" world. For most survivors, going home was not a return to the normal world in the non-victims' understanding, for they lost their families, friends, and livelihoods, and so often returned to "nothing." Importantly, the survivor's healing requires not only engaging in this kind of adaptive behavior but, more positively, engaging in meaning making and receiving community support.

Myra Giberovitch, citing work by Marilyn Armour (2010), and Ely Witztum and Ruth Malkinson (2009), explains that in recent years meaning making has emerged as a principal method in addressing trauma both during and after the event. Trauma survivors make meaning in various ways: through interpersonal relations, work, volunteer activities, altruism, spirituality, creative endeavors, and involvement in social and political causes.[57] Giberovitch and others connect meaning making to control: "For Holocaust survivors, there is an added dimension: finding meaning in survival. Many survivors find a sense of purpose and meaning in life *by bearing witness to the atrocities they endured. In so doing, they control their feelings of helplessness and despair.*"[58]

Survivors also overcome feelings of powerlessness by writing memoirs, books, and articles, and participating in interviews, lectures, conferences, and documentation projects. Some survivors feel obligated to give back to their communities and look for meaningful ways to do so through, for example, intergenerational programs which "empower survivors to transcend their victim self-concept and assume roles as witnesses to history and educating the community."[59] This has a therapeutic healing effect that generates hope, meaning, and purpose in the survivors' lives, and of course these actions positively affect community.

Recall that one of the requirements for dignity/*kavod* is engaging in worthy life projects—*meaningful life projects*. Meaning making continues in second- (and even third-) generation offspring who want to learn about their (grand)parents' experiences and their family history, memorialize their (grand)parents' memories, translate their (grand)parents' memoirs, and participate with their (grand)parents in Holocaust-related activities such as conferences and lectures.[60] Relating these insights to our debate, second- and third-generation offspring who are often vicariously affected by the survivor's trauma (a topic we will revisit in the next chapter), are invested in continuing their parents' and grandparents' projects of preventing a future medical atrocity at all costs. And so even after the survivors are no longer with us, their values, projects, and concerns continue through their family members and community.

In her poem, "The Chorus of the Rescued," Nelly Sachs vividly brings to life the fragility of the self, how it was undone by the horrors of the Holocaust, and how healing requires an understanding, caring community:

> We, the rescued,
> Beg you:
> Show us your sun. . . . but gradually.
> Lead us from star to star, step by step.
> Be gentle when you teach us to live again.
> Lest the song of a bird,
> Or a pail being filled at the well,
> Let our badly sealed pain burst forth again
> And carry us away—
> We beg you:
> Do not show us an angry dog, not yet—
> It could be, it could be
> That we will dissolve into dust—
> Dissolve into dust before your very eyes.[61]

Herman tells us that the community has the power to influence the eventual outcome of the survivors' trauma. If others respond supportively to her, this might reduce the impact of the traumatic event and help hasten the healing process. By contrast, if others respond with hostility, if they outright ignore or dismiss the survivor, this compounds the damaging effects of the trauma. The survivor needs support and validation from others who will help her understand the trauma and overcome her feelings of self-blame, humiliation, and guilt. Yehuda similarly notes that an important component of treating traumatized persons is the provision of education and a feeling of safety and support.[62]

Trauma damages and often destroys relationships, including the survivor's relationship with the community. Restoring this relationship requires (1) public acknowledgment of the traumatic event, and (2) some agreed-upon form of community action to help repair the harm. Jill Stauffer explains that "a trauma survivor's sense of the self's independence has been interrupted by violence. That sense is part of what should be restored by transitional justice or reconciliative efforts."[63] We have met the first requirement (public acknowledgment), for most everyone accepts the reality of the Holocaust, and those who do not we dismiss as mad. Some might believe that we have also met the second requirement. But many survivors of Nazi experiments suggest otherwise.

The survivors recognize that their healing requires our cooperation. As Brison explains, in this sense they are similar to people living with a disability. The Nazi victims are "disabled selves," so to speak. How well the disabled function and flourish depends to a large extent on how their social and physical environments are set up. How ought we to accommodate the disabled? Shouldn't we ask them? We need to provide an environment in which they can flourish. Many survivors suggest a way in which we can help them do just that, and this ties to meaning making and engaging in worthy life projects. Many suggest that giving them control of the data would accomplish this. But this requires our cooperation to bring that about.

Many Jews recognize the importance of community. As Batya Bauman explains, "Jews, of all people, know what 'community' means, for Jews have always been a community, and the Jewish people are a community today."[64] While many Jews recognize and feel a kinship with Jews from other lands whom they have never met, they also understand that they belong to a larger community, which includes non-Jews. Their concerns about the character of community and one's responsibilities within it stretch to this extended community. If we treat members of the community like members of an extended family, then we come to care about the well-being of those members.

If a family member were harmed, most of us would care about her healing and strive to bring that about. However, Herman warns about the dangers of jumping in to help without taking the survivors' requests into account. Referring to survivors of rape and domestic violence she writes, "Family members may decide on their own course of action in the aftermath of a traumatic event and may ignore or override the survivors' wishes, *thereby once again disempowering her.*[65] Instead of restoring control to the survivor, the family's good intentions bring about harmful effects.

Healing requires a dialogue between the survivors and the larger community. Let us now focus on the survivors' side of our debate over whether we should continue using the Nazi data, or whether we should give survivors (or their surrogates) control as they request. We need to understand why survivors might believe that their healing requires controlling the data. At this stage, I will not argue that they should control the data because they are the real moral experts in our debate. I defend this claim in the final chapter.

To understand how the Holocaust survivor might arrive at the belief that she must control the Nazi data, let us review what we have learned concerning how victims heal from trauma:

1. Engaging in self-blame and guilt can be helpful and even necessary strategies for healing from trauma, especially for those most traumatized.
2. Engaging in self-blaming strategies helps to reestablish the survivor's belief in a controllable, non-random world, one in which people can control negative outcomes.
3. Believing that one can make a difference, that one can prevent future misfortunes, is very comforting.
4. When one engages in self-blame, one believes not only that one can but also that one *must* make a difference. One has a duty to protect future generations from a repeat of the trauma.

5. Those survivors who believe that they must make a difference often obsess about prevention.
6. Engaging in self-blame and obsessive behavior should diminish over time, but those most traumatized often get stuck at this stage.

We should also recall two important facts about the Holocaust survivors:

7. The Holocaust survivors are especially prone to self-blame given the setup of the camps.
8. The Holocaust survivors are among the most severely traumatized.

Let us now reconstruct what might be going on in the Holocaust survivor's inner world when she considers our debate. In engaging in this exercise, I do not presume to know what it is like to be a Holocaust survivor. I do not assume that all of the survivors' inner worlds look alike. I merely hope to gain some understanding by applying trauma experts' insights to this debate.

The Holocaust survivors, engaging in self-blaming strategies (as we have seen so many of them do) as a means to rebuild a positive, non-threatening sense of self and the world, believe that they can make a difference and prevent future harms. Many survivors speak with the confidence of someone who believes that she can make a difference. Consider the following testimony by survivor Eva Kor:

> In the case of the Mengele Twins, copies of the data should be given to those twins who are still alive. The data of the victims who are dead should be shredded and placed in a transparent monument, as evidence that they exist, but cannot be used. It should be a lesson to the world that human dignity and human life are more important than any advances in the science of medicine.[66]

Kor then proceeds to outline standards of conduct that scientists and doctors should follow to prevent them from becoming "Mengeles of today." Another survivor writes, "No dignity should be afforded to the data or to those who produced them. The data should be thrown to the wind and forgotten. No torture permits someone else's life to be saved. We can make our own discoveries without offending humanity."[67]

These survivors seem to be saying, "Give us control of the data and we will show you how to prevent future abuses." In destroying the data, or in placing them in the hands of the survivors, society announces that data gained from unethical experiments (past or future) will not be cited, despite human benefit. Those who were "subjects" in the experiments know the evil of the experiments, and they know what people are capable of doing for the sake of humankind (or better, for the sake of *their own kind*).

Perhaps in large part motivated by feelings of guilt, survivors often obsess about preventing future abuses and believe that they can help future generations in preventing this tragedy from repeating itself. This helps them alleviate these negative feelings and reconnect with humanity, while restoring their belief in a controllable world. I acknowledge that I seem to be blurring the important distinction between (1) giving survivors control so that they can decide whether and how the data might be used, and (2) prohibiting use of the data. The reason is that many survivors blur the distinction, indicating that were they given control, the data would not be used. Indeed, the data would be altogether destroyed. Of course at least some survivors, if given control of the data, would favor using the data (perhaps under restricted conditions and with appropriate disclaimers). I acknowledge that there is no universal agreement among survivors (or their children and grandchildren who are invested in continuing the memories and projects of their (grand) parents). However, I can only work with the testimony that is available, and most of those who have been vocal, including those whom I interviewed on my trip to Israel, argue that survivors should have control and the data should not be used.

Survivors' words tend to be very passionate. Passion can be mistaken for irrationality. People who are very passionate about a topic are often considered to be irrational. We saw the survivor who, at the 1989 international conference, was criticized for being "ruled by emotions and not by the mind." Yet irrationality is not a necessary component of passion. Someone can be passionate without at all being irrational. Passion often reflects a deep commitment to one's beliefs and projects.

How does the survivors' need to control the data connect with dignity? On my account, dignity requires control (especially in the sense of self-determination), societal acknowledgment of value (since society has the power to grant or deny control), and living a life worthy of pursuit (which requires acting morally and responsibly). The survivors want to prevent future (medical) atrocities and make the community a better place. This is a worthy life goal. This also connects with meaning making, which has beneficial therapeutic effects. The proliferation of Holocaust memoirs and other writings shows the large number of survivors working toward the end of prevention. Many survivors believe that they must control the data to help accomplish this. They have made their views known, yet researchers continue to use the data.

Survivors have a clear sense of what they would do with the data were they or their surrogates given control. Many believe that they must destroy the data to prevent future Mengeles. However, they are not in positions of power such that they can just take the data. I recognize that in wording it in this way, I seem to suggest that the data is gathered together in a giant box in some warehouse and can easily be taken to the incinerator. Of course I do not intend this, and I recognize that "taking the data" is extremely complicated. On the survivors' view, preventing them from having control of the data (using the data without their consent) counts as harm, because we prevent them from engaging in this worthy goal. Further (and I will articulate how in the next chapter), when we continue to use the data without their consent, we continue to use them, and we harm ourselves and our community.

Survivors (or their surrogates) cannot accomplish their goal so long as we maintain control. Of course there is a practical problem with giving them control since the data has found its way into numerous journals and much of our science is built on Nazi data. But should we decide to honor their request, we can give survivors or their surrogates control of the originals (should they still exist), and prevent future citations of the data.

Someone might suggest that we should approach the survivors' healing in a different manner. Might there be a therapist who advocates complete disassociation from the trauma, whose aim is the survivor's daily functioning—"getting through each day," rather than insist that the survivor confront her past and work toward future prevention? Of course I acknowledge the theoretical possibility of such a therapist, but she would be a bad therapist indeed. Yehuda explains that recovery from trauma involves confronting human vulnerability in a way that promotes the development of resilience. However, the biological responses in the aftermath of trauma might perpetuate a state of fear that interferes with the restoration of safety. Living in a state of perpetual fear can overwhelm a person's coping resources and lead her to avoid thoughts and feelings associated with the trauma. Even so,

> Avoidance reduces opportunities to extinguish or diminish fear responses—for example, through exposure to information that could correct exaggerated beliefs about the safety of the world and the fragility of the person—and prevents the development of effective coping strategies, resulting in further social, interpersonal, or occupational disruption.[68]

Lancaster et al. write that one of the most empirically supported treatments for trauma survivors experiencing PTSD is so-called exposure-based therapies in which the therapist helps the patient to systematically approach, instead of avoid, safe but feared stimuli (such as trauma memories) in the absence of feared consequences (such as bodily harm or unending anxiety) until the feared consequences are disconfirmed and the automatic fear response to the trauma-related stimuli subsides.[69] Yehuda similarly remarks, "Although many traumatized persons attempt to avoid distressing emotions related to their experiences, being able to confront them will promote habituation, so that over time, their thoughts about and emotional responses to the event will become less distressing."[70] Jessica Hamblen et al. of the National Center for PTSD, agree that exposure-based therapies in which the survivor repeatedly re-experiences her traumatic event without becoming overwhelmed prove very effective in treating PTSD.[71] I want to work within the framework of current, accepted theories of trauma. Engaging in avoidance behavior is simply not the way to recover. It goes against all that we currently understand about trauma and recovery.

Traditionally, Western psychology and psychiatry have regarded disassociation as maladaptive, as interfering with the survivor's accurate perception of reality—and having an accurate perception of reality is necessary for mental health. Avoidance or outright denial of the trauma in the short run might protect the survivor from overwhelming emotions, and it might be useful and valuable in the short run for that reason. This enables the survivor to gradually, and so manageably, confront and incorporate her victimization. However, avoidance of the trauma should only be for the short term. So the therapist who advocates complete disassociation from the trauma works against the survivor's recovery.

I have argued that survivors believe that they should control the data in large part to alleviate their feelings of self-blame and guilt (this need not be conscious). Importantly, survivors concern themselves with alleviating *past* guilt. That is, they do not seem as concerned about any future guilt they might feel about future deaths caused by *not* using the data. Probably most survivors are not aware of this. Alleviating feelings of guilt and self-blame requires "setting things right," engaging in projects that "make up" for what the person has "done." Clearly the survivors (and their descendants, who continue their projects) see a strong link between destroying, and henceforth ignoring, the data and preventing future wrongs. We have also seen how the survivors' project connects with meaning making, which also works toward their healing and making the community a better place. Is it reasonable to think that we could (or should) talk survivors out of their beliefs?

According to many therapists, survivors must go through this stage of self-blame and guilt, which requires engaging in controlling behaviors to help alleviate these feelings. But therapists must also show survivors that their feelings are not ultimately justified. If therapists can show survivors that these feelings, while initially a component of their healing, are not justified (that their need to control the data is grounded in unwarranted guilt), that undermines controlling the data *for this reason*. However, there might be other reasons that they should control the data, especially if (1) the data is a part of their selves and so rightly belongs to them, and (2) they are the real experts in the debate who understand the data's true meaning and the harm we cause to survivors, their descendants, and our community when we use it. I look at these reasons in the next two chapters.

One might argue that while denying survivors control of the data prevents them from working through their guilt, there might be other ways to accomplish this. The therapist can teach the survivor strategies and skills to help her confront and reappraise the trauma. Further, another might say, there might be other ways to engage in meaning making besides controlling the data. When therapists work to alleviate the survivors' feelings of self-blame and guilt, this does not require doing what they say, just as my helping a friend get through a troubling time does not require my doing what she says—especially if what she requests is immoral, unreasonable, or too costly. Suppose that survivors say that we must kill present-day Germans, rather than give them control of the data. Obviously we would not want to do what survivors say in this case. To resolve this, we must look at dignity/*kavod* and what it means to have it. To have dignity/*kavod* includes engaging in worthy life projects and acting morally responsible. Although we might not be able to specify exactly what this means, we can rule out certain acts as being unworthy and morally irresponsible. So were survivors to say that they are engaging in a worthy life project by ridding the world of "evil Germans," we could confidently reply that they are wrong.

Someone might also object that we ought not to do what survivors say, since the survivors' response is a manifestation of an understandable, but nonetheless pathological, inability to empathize with others in need. Or perhaps their extreme reactions of bitterness, rage, or utter indifference to the future suffering of others arise out of their feelings of complete helplessness and a desire to restore their own sense of power. While the survivors' desire is understandable (since, after all, restoring control is necessary for dignity) *their way of going about it is perverted.* While I acknowledge these possibilities, I will build the case that, far from having a perverted understanding of our debate (as people have claimed), the survivors are the only ones who properly comprehend it.

Being motivated solely by self-blame and guilt leads to approaching the debate from an emotionally crippling perspective, since these feelings direct moral judgment. As we have seen, survivors reject others' assessment of them as "emotional cripples." If indeed the survivors are experts in our debate, then this negative assessment is unjustified and even harmful. Even if survivors work through their guilt, they might still want to engage in the worthy project of preventing future unethical experiments. Further, they might still believe that the best way to accomplish this is by destroying the data—especially if the data is, as they claim, *evil.* Finally, if we do not give survivors control of the data, not only do we work against their healing, but we also continue to harm them, their descendants, and our community.

NOTES

1. Charles Taylor, *Sources of the Self: The Making of Modern Identity* (Cambridge, MA: Harvard University Press, 1989), 28.
2. Lawrence Langer, *Holocaust Testimonies* (New Haven, CT: Yale University Press, 1991), 200.
3. Dan Pagis, "Draft of a Reparations Agreement," in *Holocaust Poetry*, ed. Hilda Schiff (New York: St. Martin's Press, 1996), 132.
4. David Rousset, "The Dead Stars Pursue their Courses," in *Holocaust: Religious and Philosophical Implications*, eds. John Roth and Michael Berenbaum (St. Paul, MN: Paragon House, 1989), 234, my emphasis.
5. Judith Herman, *Trauma and Recovery: The Aftermath of Violence—From Domestic Abuse to Political Terror* (New York: Basic Books, 1997), 5.
6. Cynthia Lancaster et al., "Posttraumatic Stress Disorder: Overview of Evidence Based Assessment and Treatment," *Journal of Clinical Medicine* 5, no. 11 (November 2016). See also Rachel Yehuda, "Posttraumatic Stress Disorder," *The New England Journal of Medicine* (January 2002): 108–14.
7. Lawrence Langer, *Holocaust Testimonies* (New Haven, CT: Yale University Press, 1991), 97.
8. Judith Herman, *Trauma and Recovery: The Aftermath of Violence—From Domestic Abuse to Political Terror* (New York: Basic Books, 1997), 160.
9. Bernard Gotfryd, "Reunions," in *Images from the Holocaust: A Literature Anthology*, eds. Jean Brown et al. (Lincolnwood, IL: NTC Publishing Group, 1996), 404
10. Bessie K., in Lawrence Langer, *Holocaust Testimonies* (New Haven, CT: Yale University Press, 1991), 49.
11. Elie Wiesel, "An Exchange," with Richard Rubenstein, in *Holocaust: Religious and Philosophical Implications*, eds. John Roth and Michael Berenbaum (St. Paul, MN: Paragon House, 1989), 363.
12. Judith Herman, *Trauma and Recovery: The Aftermath of Violence—From Domestic Abuse to Political Terror* (New York: Basic Books, 1997), 51.
13. Lawrence Thomas, "The Grip of Immorality," in *Reason, Ethics, and Society*, ed. J. B. Schneewind (Chicago: Open Court Press, 1996), 150.
14. *Ibid.*, 152.
15. *Ibid.*, 153.
16. Cynthia Lancaster et al., "Posttraumatic Stress Disorder: Overview of Evidence Based Assessment and Treatment," *Journal of Clinical Medicine* 5, no. 11 (November 2016).
17. Rachel Yehuda, "Posttraumatic Stress Disorder," *The New England Journal of Medicine* (January 2002): 108–14.
18. Judith Herman, *Trauma and Recovery: The Aftermath of Violence—From Domestic Abuse to Political Terror* (New York: Basic Books, 1997), 57.
19. E. M. Broner, *A Weave of Women* (Bloomington: Indiana University Press, 1985), 258–59.
20. *Ibid.*, 259.

21. Judith Herman, *Trauma and Recovery: The Aftermath of Violence—From Domestic Abuse to Political Terror* (New York: Basic Books, 1997), 93, my emphasis.

22. Rachel Brenner, "Teaching the Holocaust in the Academia: Educational Mission(s) and Pedagogical Approaches," *Journal of Holocaust Education* 8, no. 2 (1999): 4.

23. Charlotte Delbo, *Auschwitz and After*, trans. Rosette C. Lamont (New Haven, CT: Yale University Press, 1995), 247.

24. See Lawrence Langer, *Holocaust Testimonies* (New Haven, CT: Yale University Press, 1991), 91.

25. Judith Herman, *Trauma and Recovery: The Aftermath of Violence—From Domestic Abuse to Political Terror* (New York: Basic Books, 1997), 83.

26. Simone De Beauvoir, *The Second Sex*, trans. H. M. Parshley (New York: Random House, 1952), 451.

27. *Ibid.*, 84.

28. Tadeusz Borowski, *This Way for the Gas, Ladies and Gentleman*, trans. Barbara Vedder and Michael Kandel (New York: Penguin Classics, 1992), 32.

29. Hannah Arendt, *Origins of Totalitarianism* (New York: Harcourt Brace Jovanovich, 1952), 447, my emphasis.

30. J. M. Bernstein, *Torture and Dignity: An Essay on Moral Injury* (Chicago: University of Chicago Press, 2015), 278, emphasis in the original.

31. Lawrence Langer, "The Dilemma of Choice," in *Holocaust: Religious and Philosophical Implications*, eds. John Roth and Michael Berenbaum (St. Paul, MN: Paragon House, 1989), 231.

32. Tadeusz Borowski, *This Way for the Gas, Ladies and Gentleman*, trans. Barbara Vedder and Michael Kandel (New York: Penguin Classics, 1992), 35.

33. Elie Wiesel, *Night*, trans. Stella Rodway (New York: Bantam Books, 1986), 61.

34. Lawrence Langer, *Holocaust Testimonies* (New Haven, CT: Yale University Press, 1991), 87.

35. Calel Perechodnik, *Am I a Murderer? Testament of a Jewish Ghetto Policeman*, ed. and trans. Frank Fox (Boulder, CO: Westview Press, 1996), 9.

36. Claudia Card, *The Unnatural Lottery: Character and Moral Luck* (Philadelphia: Temple University Press, 1996), 7.

37. David Jones, *Moral Responsibility in the Holocaust* (Lanham, MD: Rowman & Littlefield, 1999), 75.

38. John Roth, "Reflections on Post-Holocaust Ethics," in *Problems Unique to the Holocaust*, ed. Harry James Cargas (Lexington: The University Press of Kentucky, 1999), 170.

39. Ronnie Janoff-Bulman, *Shattered Assumptions: Towards a New Psychology of Trauma* (New York: Free Press, 1992), 7, 9.

40. *Ibid.*, 14.

41. Yehuda Bauer, *A History of the Holocaust* (Danbury, CT: Franklin Watts Press, 1982), 247.

42. Elie Wiesel, *Night*, trans. Stella Rodway (New York: Bantam Books, 1986), 42.

43. Quoted in Ronnie Janoff-Bulman, *Shattered Assumptions: Towards a New Psychology of Trauma* (New York: Free Press, 1992), 61.

44. Rachel Yehuda, "Posttraumatic Stress Disorder," *The New England Journal of Medicine* (January 2002): 108–14.

45. Ronnie Janoff-Bulman, *Shattered Assumptions: Towards a New Psychology of Trauma* (New York: Free Press, 1992), 63.

46. Isabella Leitner, "Saving the Fragments," in *Images from the Holocaust: A Literature Anthology*, eds. Jean Brown et al. (Lincolnwood, IL: NTC Publishing Group, 1996), 410.

47. Judith Herman, *Trauma and Recovery: The Aftermath of Violence—From Domestic Abuse to Political Terror* (New York: Basic Books, 1997), 159.

48. *Ibid.*, 206, my emphasis.

49. Irving Feldman, "To the Six Million," in *Truth and Lamentation*, eds. Milton Teichman and Sharon Leder (Chicago: University of Illinois Press, 1994), 461ff., my emphasis.

50. H. Leivick, "I Hear a Voice," in *Truth and Lamentation*, eds. Milton Teichman and Sharon Leder (Chicago: University of Illinois Press, 1994), 472.

51. Bertolt Brecht, "I, the Survivor," in *Holocaust Poetry*, ed. Hilda Schiff (New York: St. Martin's Press, 1996), 127.

52. Rachel Yehuda, "Posttraumatic Stress Disorder," *The New England Journal of Medicine* (January 2002): 108–14.

53. *Ibid.*, 128.

54. Lawrence Langer, *Holocaust Testimonies* (New Haven, CT: Yale University Press, 1991), 185.

55. *Ibid.*, 187.

56. *Ibid.*, 32–33.

57. Myra Giberovitch, *Recovering from Genocidal Trauma: An Information and Practice Guide for Working with Holocaust Survivors* (Toronto: University of Toronto Press, 2014), 95.

58. *Ibid.*, 95–96, my emphasis.

59. *Ibid.*, 194.

60. *Ibid.*, 99.

61. Nelly Sachs, "Chorus of the Rescued," in *Art from the Ashes: A Holocaust Anthology*, ed. Lawrence L. Langer (New York: Oxford University Press, 1995), 643.

62. Rachel Yehuda, "Posttraumatic Stress Disorder," *The New England Journal of Medicine* (January 2002): 108–14.

63. Jill Stauffer, *Ethical Loneliness: The Injustice of Not Being Heard* (New York: Columbia University Press, 2015), 24.

64. Batya Bauman, "Women-Identified Women in Male-Identified Judaism," in *On Being a Jewish Feminist*, ed. Susannah Heschel (New York: Schocken Books, 1982), 88.

65. Judith Herman, *Trauma and Recovery: The Aftermath of Violence—From Domestic Abuse to Political Terror* (New York: Basic Books, 1997), 65, my emphasis.

66. Eva Kor, "Nazi Experiments as Viewed by a Survivor of Mengele's Experiments," in *When Medicine Went Mad: Bioethics and the Holocaust*, ed. Arthur Caplan (Totowa, NJ: Humana Press, 1992), 7.

67. Gisela Konopka, "The Meaning of the Holocaust for Bioethics," in *When Medicine Went Mad: Bioethics and the Holocaust*, ed. Arthur Caplan (Totowa, NJ: Humana Press, 1992), 17.

68. Rachel Yehuda, "Posttraumatic Stress Disorder," *The New England Journal of Medicine* (January 2002): 108–14.

69. Cynthia Lancaster et al., "Posttraumatic Stress Disorder: Overview of Evidence Based Assessment and Treatment," *Journal of Clinical Medicine* 5, no. 11 (November 2016).

70. Rachel Yehuda, "Posttraumatic Stress Disorder," *The New England Journal of Medicine* (January 2002): 108–14.

71. Jessica Hamblen et al., "Overview of Psychotherapy for PTSD," at ptsd.va.gov.

Chapter 5

Nazi Data

Transparent, Evil, and Transparently Evil

In this chapter, I consider two of the survivors more controversial claims: (1) they are the "living data," and so when we use the data, we use them, and (2) the data is (*truly*, not merely symbolically) evil, and we become morally tainted when we use it. In order to accomplish this, we first need to arrive at a conception of the self and its relationship to cultural objects that will help explain the victims' relationship to the Nazi data. I suggest a Merleau-Pontian (phenomenological) approach, articulated in his *Phenomenology of Perception,* which offers a conception of the self that contrasts sharply with the disembodied Cartesian thinking thing. On this view, my body is not "objective," but "phenomenal." The so-called objective body, such as Descartes conceives it, is merely a conceptual existence.[1] By contrast, the phenomenal body extends out into the world of objects and other subjects, a world saturated with meaning. As I explain, the Nazi data is a cultural object and as such it is a "meaning carrier." The data is also a temporal object, in which past selves and past experiences are (implicitly) present. Insofar as the data is both a cultural and temporal object, the victims' selves extend to the data. Indeed, as we will see, this helps explain survivor Susan Vigorito's claim at the 1989 conference that she is the "living data." When we use the data, we use the survivors—albeit more remotely and indeterminately.

One may immediately suggest that there is really nothing to explain when Vigorito calls herself the living data, for this claim is commonsensical: it reminds us that the data is not merely a collection of numbers, charts, and graphs on a page, but arises from the victims' traumatic past. What I propose is far more ambitious and contentious—even counterintuitive. While I certainly agree that survivors mean to draw attention to the data's savage history, and calling themselves the living data certainly accomplishes that, I want to argue for this stronger claim, suggesting that survivors have a richer understanding of the self's relationship to the world in virtue of their experiences.

On a Merleau-Pontian account, I give objects meaning. But other people also give meaning to objects just like I do. So an object often confronts me with meaning that it already possesses. I argue that an object's "true" meaning is revealed when we pay "proper" attention. One way to pay proper attention is via our emotions since, as Peter Goldie argues, "emotions can reveal saliences that we might not otherwise recognize with the same speed and reliability."[2]

I contend that the survivors are paying proper attention (especially given their proximity to the data), and their emotions signal the data's true meaning and its relevance to our debate. Goldie notes that emotions can also "skew the epistemic landscape." Indeed, entire communities can be wrong in their assessment.[3] I suggest that the so-called experts in our debate, the researchers and medical ethicists, have epistemically skewed landscapes because their "expertise" and "cool rationality" get in the way of paying proper attention to the data's true meaning.

As we will see, objects solicit a response from me, "beckoning me" to respond in a certain way. When I interact with objects, especially habitually, they become a part or extension of me. And so my *self* extends into the world of objects and other selves. When we interact with cultural (and temporal) objects we become aware of other selves, including other past selves. And so when we interact with the Nazi data we become aware of the victims of the experiments—that is, if we pay proper attention.

I will also argue that when we interact with the data (by using it) we incorporate it into our selves. One consequence of this view is that when we use the data we harm our community, and so the harm that originated in the Nazi camps is in nowise "over and done," nor limited to the victims, but continues into the present and affects everyone. I will need to answer objections, including that I make the conception of the self "meaningless" or "incoherent," since on this view the self seems to "carry the whole world." I explain how we can make sense of this conception by bringing in Merleau-Ponty's notion of the world horizon.

Of course an object often carries "competing" meanings and harm can come about when we inscribe an object in ways that result in the "effacement" of a past event or the "erasure" of death—what Cathy Caruth calls a kind of moral betrayal.[4] As Caruth explains, this happens when we introduce a "language of fiction" into the object's "narrative." In light of this, I need to answer another objection; namely, if an object's meanings can be multifarious and conflicting, why should we privilege one meaning over others? To answer this, I discuss the "politics" of meaning inscription. Next, I briefly address a possible concern about transitivity: If the data is evil, and survivors are the "living data," then we seem to arrive at the impossible conclusion that the survivors are evil. Finally, I answer perhaps the most "damning" objection; namely, that while it makes sense to say that victims are metaphorically present in the data, they are not literally present, and there are similar worries about evil. Evil is not literally a contaminant.

Merleau-Ponty writes that the social and cultural world is "the permanent field or dimension of existence."[5] We already find ourselves situated and engaged in it. We cannot escape it. We can turn away from it, but we cannot cease to be situated in relation to it. The social is an unavoidable dimension of our being. It is already there when we come to know it and judge it. In interacting with cultural objects, I experience the presence of others—others interacting in the world as I do, others who have also imbued objects with meaning. That is, I live in a world of intersubjective meaning. When an object confronts me with meaning that it already possesses, it invites me to respond to it in a particular way. I react to and with it. Merleau-Ponty explains that "the visual thing (the bluish disc of the moon) or the tactile thing (my head such as I sense it by palpating it) . . . [is] that which is met with or taken up by our gaze or by our movement, a question to which they respond precisely." Thus there is "a certain type of symbiosis, a certain manner that the outside has of invading us, a certain manner that we have of receiving it.[6]

Oftentimes, objects announce their meaning without my being able to say what exactly in the objects signify that meaning. The only way to understand a particular object's meaning is by interacting with it, and then its meaning is revealed. For example, consider the meaning of love in a bouquet of flowers. Merleau-Ponty writes, "It is evident that the bouquet is a bouquet of love and yet it is impossible to say what in the bouquet signifies love."[7]

When I interact with a particular object, it regulates my body's habits and orientation. As Merleau-Ponty explains, when I interact with an object, it becomes incorporated into my self as a part or extension of me, as a "present and real part of my body."[8] I do not apprehend it as an object with an "objective" location. Rather, I integrate the object and it contributes to my composition. As Merleau-Ponty explains, when I interact with the object, my body "allows itself to be penetrated by a new signification."[9] In this way, my body includes meanings that I do not constitute.

On this view, I do not stop at my "body-container."[10] To understand this, consider that the blind man's cane, for example, ceases to be an object for him. Instead, the blind man "takes up residence" in the cane and makes it "participate within the voluminosity" of the blind man's body.[11] As Merleau-Ponty describes it, "The cane is no longer an object that the blind man would perceive. . . . It is an appendage of the body, or an extension of the bodily synthesis."[12]

Similarly, when I type on my laptop, I literally incorporate the space of the keyboard into my bodily space. That is, when I type, I do not look at my fingers tapping each of the letters on the keyboard. My fingers know how to navigate the space. The keyboard becomes an extension of myself in much the same way that the blind man's cane becomes an extension of him. Merleau-Ponty explains that my relationship with the keyboard is no different from my relationship with my knee. He writes, "When I bring my hand toward my knee, I experience at each moment of the movement the realization of an intention that did not aim at my knee as an idea, or even an object, but rather as a present and real part of my living body, and ultimately as a point of passage in my perceptual movement toward a world."[13]

Interacting with cultural objects gives me a sense of other people. I feel the presence of other selves—including other *past selves*. To get a sense of this, consider the following. A couple summers ago I went on an incredible hike outside of Leadville, Colorado. It was to a little ghost town at 12,000 feet at the foot of Fletcher Mountain. In the later nineteenth century, prospectors constructed the town to mine the mountain-bound gold. It turned out to be a bust. Hiking up to the ghost town, I was surrounded by colorful wildflowers and the amazing views of the Ten Mile Range. Taken in by the surroundings, I all but forgot that I was hiking to some ruins. But then I suddenly stumbled upon the shambles of mining cabins that lined both sides of the trail. Stepping inside one of the cabins to take a photograph, I felt the presence of other people—other people long gone.

Merleau-Ponty explains that cultural objects might be only vaguely determined. In this case, we have some sense of another person without knowing many details, such as when I see footprints in the sand.[14] We may be able to determine, by the size of the footprints, that they belong to an adult rather than a child, but beyond that bit of detail we really do not know much. This is true too when we explore the ruins of an ancient civilization or an unknown foreign culture whose artifacts are unfamiliar to us—or when I came upon the mining cabins from times past. But cultural objects can also be much more determinate.

When I interact with cultural objects, I become aware of other selves in one of two ways: either as subjects or as objects. As Komarine Romdenh-Romluc explains, "When I am aware of someone as an object, I am aware of what is in fact another person, but my experience of them does not present them as significantly different from inanimate items like tables and rocks."[15] Consider, for example, looking at someone's brain activity on an MRI scan. The object of my awareness is another self, namely, the person whose brain scan I am viewing. After all, that brain scan would not exist were it not for another person—*that person*—having had an MRI. Even though I am in fact experiencing another person, my experience of that person is on a par with my awareness of things such as cars and coffee cups.[16]

The Nazi data is incontrovertibly a cultural object. Like the MRI scan the data could not have been created without human involvement. The Nazi doctors performed medical experiments on their victims and the data was generated as a result. In the same way that I am aware of another self in viewing the brain scan, I am aware of other selves—*other tortured selves*—when interacting with the data.

Remember that my hike to the ghost town showed that the object of my awareness might be of people who are long gone. Many of the Holocaust victims are gone, and those who are still alive will not be with us much longer— *yet they are still present in the data.* They will forever be present in the data. When on my hike and I suddenly came upon the shambles of mining cabins, I could imagine what the people were doing. I could imagine them stoking a fire, perhaps preparing a big pot of stew after a long day of frustratingly futile mining. When I come upon the data, I also encounter other selves, and I can imagine, albeit imperfectly and indeterminately, what the victims must have gone through—the terror, horror, and excruciating pain.

The data has meaning—meaning created in the torturous experiments. What meaning do we discover when we interact with the data? Like the bouquet of flowers, it announces its meaning. Importantly, its meaning is only evident when we pay proper attention. As I will argue, when we fail to be sensitive to the human history implicit in the data, treating it as unproblematically usable, as some researchers seem to be doing, we miscognize it. Thus our moral error is grounded in a cognitive error.

The data is saturated in evil. *Evil* is the meaning of the data (the data, we might say, "carries" it). And yet like the bouquet of flowers, where it is impossible to say what in the bouquet signifies love, it is impossible to say what in the data signifies evil. After all, the data is nothing more (and yet so much more) than a collection of numbers, charts, graphs, statistics, descriptions, "facts," and so on. Contrast this with the Cartesian account, in which the data is only—and nothing more than—data. That is, the Cartesian account fails to make present the evil.

When I engage the data, as researchers do when they pore over it, it confronts me with this meaning that it already possesses—*this meaning of evil*— and it beckons me to respond to it in a particular way. How do we respond to evil? Certainly we should not respond to it by reinscribing its meaning in the way that Caruth describes—by erasing the suffering and death.

When I interact with the data, especially as I become more familiar with it, I incorporate it—I allow my body (my self) to be penetrated by this new signification. While I do not relate to the data in the same way that a blind man relates to his cane or I relate to my keyboard, I nonetheless take on the data's meaning, and in so doing I implicate myself in the evil. This is inescapable since I live in a deeply social world. I am intimately connected to others (including past others) and to their activities and experiences. And the data bears the mark of these activities and experiences.

Before I continue, I should pause to say a few words about evil, since it plays such a significant role in my arguments. "Evil" is a charged term, and although I need not be committed to a particular conception to get my points across (especially since I believe that we all share pretty good intuitions here), I am most inclined to accept Claudia Card's definition, which she defends in her work *The Atrocity Paradigm*. Card writes,

> [E]vils are foreseeable intolerable harms produced by culpable wrongdoing. On my theory, the nature and severity of the harms, rather than perpetrators' psychological states, distinguish evils from ordinary wrongs. Evils tend to ruin lives, or significant parts of lives. It is not surprising if victims never recover or are never quite able to move on, although sometimes people do recover and move on. Evildoers, however, are not necessarily malicious. Oftener they are inexcusably reckless, callously indifferent, amazingly unscrupulous. Evildoers need not be evil people, although they may become so over time.[17]

One way to get a sense of how we become implicated in the evil when we use the data is to look at J. M. Coetzee's novel *Elizabeth Costello*. On one of her lectures around the world, (fictitious) celebrated writer Elizabeth Costello goes to Amsterdam and gives a lecture on the topic of evil, in which she talks about (real) writer Paul West's novel, *The Very Rich Hours of Count von Stauffenberg*. Stauffenberg was the leading member of the July 1944 failed plot to assassinate Hitler. Speaking to the audience which, as luck would have it, includes West, Costello explains, "I ought to read to you from these terrible pages, but I will not, because I do not believe it will be good for you or for me to hear them. I even assert (and here I come to the point) that I do not believe it was good for Mr. West, if he will forgive my saying so, to write those pages."[18]

Costello explains that the artist risks a great deal by venturing into forbidden places: risks to himself and, indeed, risks to all of us. A man from the audience challenges Costello's words: "How do you know that Mr. West . . . has been harmed by what he has written? If I understand you correctly, you are saying that if you yourself had written this book about Stauffenberg and Hitler you would have been infected with the Nazi evil."[19] Costello replies, "Mr. West, when he wrote those chapters, came in touch with something absolute. Absolute evil. . . . *Through reading him that touch of evil was passed on to me*. . . . *It is not something that can be demonstrated*."[20] I imagine that this is what the survivors are getting at when they suggest that we become morally tainted by our contact with the data. Of course we cannot see it—we are not covered in black goo, for example. But we are tainted by evil nonetheless.

Nicolle Jordan similarly argues that evil is a moral contagion. In her essay, "A Creole Contagion: Narratives of Slavery and Tainted Wealth in *Millennium Hall*," Jordan discusses Sarah Scott's 1762 novel about a utopian community on a remote Cornwall estate founded by six women devoted to philanthropy. The community is supported by colonial wealth. Jordan argues that "the novel offers evidence of Scott's apprehension that colonial wealth may be deeply tainted. It may be a source of moral contagion."[21] Scott's belief that colonial wealth entails moral contagion is seen in her suggestion that colonial wealth, acquired by the slave labor of the colonies, compromises the health of the men who earned it. As Jordan argues, Scott suggests that where money comes from is just as important as what one does with it. Morally tainted colonial wealth thus compromises the virtuous mission of Millennium Hall; it infiltrates and infects.

As I argued above, the Nazi data is a cultural object saturated in evil. The evil is historical, and thus temporal. I now argue that the data is also a temporal object, or alternatively: a temporal object nested inside a cultural object. I explain what I mean.

To understand what Merleau-Ponty means by "temporal object," we should first briefly consider his conception of time. On his account, the past and future are implicitly present in the "now." We can see what he means by considering his analogy with perception, which is necessarily of a figure against a background. The figure is the focus of our attention, which stands out from a background, which we perceive indeterminately. Romdenh-Romluc explains Merleau-Ponty's account in this way:

> The world and the subject that precede perception can figure in our experience without being perceived. Indeed, they figure in *all* our experience.... Perceiving is an ongoing process of making the indeterminate and ambiguous determinate.... The indeterminacy of what is seen increases with the distance to such an extent that one's awareness of the furthest region of the background is simply the experience of a vast presence, continuing indefinitely into the distance.[22]

Certain things, namely those that are the focus of my attention, are presented explicitly. Other things are implicitly present—they remain indeterminate and ambiguous in the background. In other words, the background is implicitly presented in my current experience; it is hidden, but co-present. Indeed, I am implicitly presented with the whole world, although the indeterminacy and ambiguity are so great that I only experience it as a massive presence.[23]

Suppose that I hold a coffee cup and I cover a part of it. I explicitly see the parts that are not covered. However, I am implicitly presented with the hidden parts. I experience the hidden parts of the cup as co-present with the parts that I explicitly see. Or imagine that I look at a lamp on my table. As Merleau-Ponty explains,

> I attribute to it not merely the qualities that are visible from my location, but those also that the fireplace, the walls, and the table can "see." . . . Thus, I can see one object insofar as objects form a system or a world, and insofar as each of them arranges the others around itself like spectators of its hidden aspects and as the guarantee of their permanence.[24]

Temporal objects are like this. An object is "seen" from all times just as it is seen from all places. According to Merleau-Ponty, "Whatever is past or future for me is present in the world. . . . Past and future exist all too well in the world, *they exist in the present.*"[25] Merleau-Ponty introduces Husserl's conceptions of "retention" and "protention" to refer to our implicit awareness of what one *has* experienced, and what one *will* experience, respectively. He describes the implicit presentation of the past and its retentions like this: "The present still holds in hand the immediate past, but without positing it as an object, and since the immediate past likewise retains the past that immediately preceded it, time gone by is entirely taken up and grasped in the present."[26]

That is, a retention is a retained experience with its own retentions, and so on. Thus a temporal object contains a "nested series" of retentions.[27] Merleau-Ponty helps us understand what he has in mind by bringing in our bodies:

> Just as it is necessarily "here," the body necessarily exists "now"; it can never become "past." Even if we cannot preserve the living memory of the illness when we are healthy, nor the living memory of our body as a child when we have become an adult, these "gaps in memory" do nothing but express the temporal structure of our body. At each moment in a movement, the preceding instant is not forgotten, but rather is somehow fit into the present.[28]

A temporal object implicitly presents stages of itself that are not present. The implicit presentation of past (and future) stages is references to experiences of that object that I could see, *or I could have seen*, from a different point in time.[29]

Just as we are aware of another person when we view an MRI scan, we are aware of the victims when we interact with the data. More specifically, we are aware of *their experiences*. An experience is a temporal object. Romdenh-Romluc writes about attending a duck race, which I have slightly amended in what follows. Most of us are familiar with a duck race, where the competitors write their names on the sides of their plastic ducks. At the sound of the whistle, they are released downstream, and the first one to cross the finish line wins. Imagine that I see the start of the duck race, but then I get a call on my cell phone and must step away. When I return, I see the winning duck just about to cross the finish line. As Romdenh-Romluc explains, "For my experience to give me a sense of the ducks as travelling along the river, it must implicitly present them as having been further upstream."[30] In other words, the implicit presentation of the ducks racing further upstream is a reference to an experience *that I could have seen*, had I not taken my phone call.

In the case of the victims' experiences, the implicit presentation of the past temporal stages is a presentation of their experiences that *I could have seen* from a different point in time (for example, had I lived in certain parts of Central Europe during World War II). Thus the victims' experiences in the camps are nested retentions of a temporal object—a temporal object that is "carried" with the data. It seems fitting then to say that the data is a temporal object (the victims' experiences) nested within a cultural object (the "facts," figures, and so on, recorded on the page). This is another way of saying that the victims are "present" in the data. Their past experiences are implicitly present, or "hidden" but co-present. If this is so, then when we use the data, we use the victims, and so this constitutes a continuation of the past harm.

We can make this even stronger by looking at psychiatrist Dori Laub's explanation of a survivor's relationship to the traumatic experience: "The traumatic event, although real, took place outside the parameters of 'normal' reality, such as causality, sequence, place, and time. The trauma is thus an event that has no beginning, no ending, no before, no during and no after."[31] This quality gives it a "salience, a timelessness, and a ubiquity." On Laub's account, the survivors' "past" experiences are not even past. That is, unlike a duck race, which has a temporal ordering—a beginning, middle, and an end—the survivors' experiences, which we find implicitly present in the data, are salient, timeless, and ubiquitous. So when we use the data, the result is not a "continuation" of a "past" harm, but an ongoing harm—a harm that has never left.

That the victims are "in" the data can also be understood by looking at Toni Morrison's *Beloved*, which Marianne Hirsch discusses. Sethe meets her mother only once: "Her mother took her behind the smokehouse, opened her dress, and showed her the mark under her breast: Right on her rib was a circle and cross burnt right in the skin. She said, 'This is your ma'am.'"[32] As Hirsch explains, "When Sethe's mother points out that 'this is your ma'am' she identifies the mother with the burned circle and cross on her skin. The mark *is* the mother—'this is your ma'am'—and it is also the vehicle for mother/daughter recognition—'you will know me by this mark.'"[33] Understood in this way, the data *is* the survivor—"I am the 'living data'"—and one of the ways we come to know the survivor is by interacting with it.

As I have explained, when we use the data we incorporate it into our selves—our bodies "allow themselves to be penetrated by a new signification." We take on the data's meaning, and in so doing we implicate ourselves in the evil. Now that we have an understanding of the data as a temporal object (or a temporal object nested inside a cultural object), we get a clearer picture of what the survivors might have in mind. Merleau-Ponty explains that "since my living present opens up to a past that I nevertheless no longer live and to a future that I do not yet live, or that I might never live, *it can also open up to temporalities that I do not live and can have a social horizon such that my world is enlarged to the extent of the collective history that my private existence takes up and carries forward.*"[34]

Recall that the figure is the focus of my attention, which stands out against an indeterminate background. Merleau-Ponty seems to suggest that *we can take up others' (past) experiences* within the "social horizon," if they become the focus of our attention. Consider, for example, Iris Murdoch's 1964 novel *The Italian Girl*. David Levkin tells the narrator, Edmund, that there are two kinds of Jews: "There are Jews that suffer and Jews that succeed, the dark Jews and the light Jews. She is a dark Jew. . . . She is all memory—she remembers so much, *she remembers the memories that are not her own.*"[35] We can also see this clearly in children of Holocaust survivors' descriptions of their relationships to their parents' memories. Hirsch discusses the memoir *The War After*, written by British journalist Anne Karpf, the daughter of an Auschwitz survivor. Karpf enumerates the bodily symptoms through which she experiences her mother's sense-memories of the camps, which include terrible eczema: "After years of my scratching, a close friend asked whether the place on my inside forearm that I was repeatedly injuring wasn't the same place, indeed the very same arm, where my mother's concentration number was inked. I was astonished—it had never occurred to me."[36] As Hirsch explains, Karpf's "relationship to her mother becomes incorporative and appropriative—more a form of 'transposition' than identification."[37]

Extensive research supports the above hypothesis that trauma can be passed to the next generation. This includes physical, behavioral, emotional, psychological, and cognitive problems, including hypertension, cardiovascular disease, anxiety, low self-esteem, inhibition of aggression, lower inhibitory control, and lower visuospatial working memory performance.[38] Indeed, Rachel Yehuda et al. in an article entitled "Relationship Between Posttraumatic Stress Disorder Characteristics of Holocaust Survivors and their Adult Offspring," cite the Holocaust survivor poet, Paul Celan, who aptly wrote that children of survivors "suckled the black milk" of trauma.[39] Mallory E. Bowers and Rachel Yehuda explain that the impetus to study so-called intergenerational transmission of stress has come from offspring of trauma survivors who have used a variety of forums, including the arts and literature, and mental health clinics, to articulate the effects of parental trauma on their own mental health.[40] As they describe, there are various mechanisms by which transmission of stress can occur, including (1) parents modeling behaviors and children learning to react to their environments in manners similar to their parents, and (2) offspring inheriting the same or similar genetic risks that have an impact on their own stress vulnerability. More recently, as a result of advances in understanding of epigenetic mechanisms, an additional hypothesis has emerged: "that offspring of severely stress-exposed parents are at risk for adverse outcomes because of enduring epigenetic changes in parental biological systems that have arisen in response to stress exposure and are transmitted" (see Yehuda and Bierer, 2009; Yehuda et al., 2014).[41] Further, at least one study suggests that stress is even transmitted to the third generation (see Scharf 2007).[42]

On a Merleau-Pontian account, when we interact with the data, it is drawn out of the background. We take up the victims' past experiences that are implicitly present in it and we "carry them forward." Thus we have not only taken on the data's meaning, but we have also taken on the victims' experiences, and so when we use the data we also use ourselves, albeit more remotely and indeterminately. We harm our community. And since, as the clinical literature shows, survivors have transmitted their trauma (in varying degrees) to their descendants who often take up their projects, we harm them too.

As I noted above, the data's true meaning is revealed when we pay proper attention. Our emotions play a role in this. I will explain what I mean. Recall that Goldie states that emotions can reveal saliences by drawing things or events to our attention. Even stronger, emotions can enable us to get things right by attuning us to the world around us, "enabling us quickly and reliably to see things as they really are, and thus to respond as we should."[43] For example, emotions can enable us to immediately see something as frightening, insulting, or disgusting in ways we would not be able to see were we not capable of experiencing emotions. When we interact with the data, we experience an admixture of anger, heartache, and pain (as well as other emotions), which thus signals us to the data's true meaning and our appropriate responses to it. Indeed, only someone who would approach the data cool-heartedly, shutting off her emotions, would miss the data's true meaning. Recall Vigorito's words from the 1989 conference: "I have been in this room for two days. Everyone has spoken about data, data, data. It's the most sterile word. You are looking at the data, the living data, of Dr. Mengele. This is the data. It is my experience." It seems clear by Vigorito's statement that the conference participants had been speaking about the data cool-heartedly, sterilely. It is no wonder, then, that they missed the data's true meaning—the meaning of evil.

Goldie develops an account of emotions that makes sense of two intuitions: (1) by directing our attention, emotions can sometimes tell us things about the world that reason alone would miss, but also (2) emotions can profoundly distort our view of things. This first intuition has been corroborated in recent research by neuroscientist Patrik Vuilleumier et al.[44] The second intuition is especially relevant, since survivors have been accused of being emotional cripples who do not properly understand our debate. Goldie tells us that emotions can skew the epistemic landscape by making it cohere with our emotional experience: we seek out and find reasons that supposedly justify what is in reality unjustifiable. He explains that typically when we respond to something emotionally in our environment, and when we perceive that object as having an "emotion-proper property," we also take the emotion and the perception to be reasonable or justified.[45]

Michael Brady similarly notes that emotions capture and consume our attention. He explains what he means: "To say that attention is captured and consumed by emotional objects and events is to say that such objects and events hold sway over us, often making it difficult to disengage our attention and shift focus elsewhere." Brady argues that we should not take our emotional appraisals at face value. He explains that emotions can keep our attention fixed on the object or event that elicited the emotions, and in so doing they can motivate us to search for and discover reasons that bear on the accuracy of our initial evaluation of the object or event. That is, the emotional capture of attention motivates reflection on the emotion itself. Thus the epistemic goal is what Brady calls "evaluative understanding" of the emotional object or event.[46]

Goldie argues that we are typically justified on the basis of our emotional experience in taking the object to have the emotion-proper property that we take it to have. However, factors can interfere with our emotional response on occasion, which cause us to fail to get things right. For example, my irritable mood, perhaps caused by drinking too much coffee, can result in my getting angry and taking someone's words to be insulting when in fact they are not. Martha Nussbaum similarly writes that "emotions can, of course, be unreliable—in much the same way that beliefs can. People can get angry because of false beliefs about the facts, or their importance; the relevant beliefs might also be true but unjustified, or both false and unjustified."[47] As she explains, emotions can be unjustified or false, just as beliefs can be.

Goldie notes that our emotions, and our emotionally held perceptual judgments about things or events as having emotion-proper properties, are more intransigent than their nonemotional counterparts. Thus, our epistemic landscape "tends to be towards the preservation of the emotionally held *idée fixes* at the cost of unemotional thoughts."[48] And so while our emotionally held perceptual judgments ought to be open to being shown to be wrong by new evidence, when new evidence does emerge we are often insensitive to it, and for the sake of internal coherence we doubt the reliability of the source of the new evidence.

In our case, I take this to be some of the 1989 conference participants' "sin." They were confronted with new evidence (the survivors' testimony), which should at the very least give them pause to reconsider their judgments, and yet in the interest of preserving their beliefs, and the value of upholding knowledge at all costs, they dismiss the survivors as emotional cripples tied to the past. They do not seek true evaluative understanding, and their "emotion" of "cool rationality" (should we call it an emotion; it certainly seems as intransigent as any "real" emotion) prevents them from engaging in this important task.

Brady rejects Goldie's presumption that we have a "default entitlement" to believe on the basis of our emotional experiences.[49] As he explains, absent the discovery of reasons to think that our emotional experiences are veridical, it is by no means obvious that we should regard ourselves as entitled to take the content of our emotional experiences at face value, as themselves reasons or evidence for our evaluative beliefs.[50] Emotions often (and should) motivate the search for reasons that bear on their accuracy, and thus on the correctness of the associated judgment. It may turn out that our emotions are reliable trackers of value, but emotional experience ought to be at best "proxies" for genuine justifying reasons. Our goal should be evaluative understanding, which can only be accomplished by subjecting our emotional responses to critical scrutiny.[51]

According to Brady, our emotions' main role is to keep our attention, which should motivate the search and discovery of reasons that bear on the accuracy of our emotions. I agree with Brady's insistence that our epistemic goal should be evaluative understanding rather than a default acceptance of our emotionally held judgment. Recall Goldie's claim that entire communities can be wrong in their evaluative assessment of an object or event. This can happen precisely when we rest content with our initial emotional judgments—judgments that are often informed by the community in which we live or work. Caruth provides a terrific example to help us appreciate this point.

In *Unclaimed Experience: Trauma, Narrative, and History,* Caruth discusses the 1959 French film *Hiroshima mon amour.* The scene opens with two alternating shots: two interlaced elbows, arms, and a hand, their sagging skin covered with ash then sweat move in a slow embrace—apparently the victims of the first atomic bombing of Hiroshima. The second shot is of two elbows, arms, and a hand, first smooth then sweaty, locked in an act of love—"an intimate encounter taking place, as we will soon discover, between a French woman and a Japanese man, who have met by chance in (post-bombing) Hiroshima."[52] Caruth asks the following question: "What do the dying bodies of the past, the dying bodies of Hiroshima, have to do with the living bodies of the present?"

This question relates to our project. Caruth discusses what she calls the "effacement" of the event of Hiroshima in the understanding of the French woman in the film, which also constitutes the understanding of Hiroshima from the perspective of national French history. In the film, the Japanese man asks the following question of the woman: "What did Hiroshima mean for you, in France?" The woman replies: "The end of the war, I mean, really the end." He responds: "The whole world was happy. You were happy with the whole world."

According to the French perspective, as Caruth explains it, Hiroshima did not signify the beginning of the suffering for the Japanese, but the end of their own suffering. The knowledge of Hiroshima was not understood as the "incomprehensible occurrence of the nuclear bombing of the Japanese," but as what they call "the end." This resulted in the effacement of the event of a Japanese past, reinscribed as a referent into the narrative of French history, which turned the Japanese catastrophe into an "anonymous narrative of peace."[53] This also brought about an "erasure of death," the false knowledge of others, and a kind of moral betrayal.

When researchers take the data to be unproblematically usable, even promoting its use, they turn the butchery so evident in the data (for those who are paying proper attention) into a collection of anonymous "facts." They take the people out of the data. This too results in an erasure of death and a moral betrayal. They certainly do not experience the anger, heartache, and pain that the data demands, for if they did they would never consider the data to be unproblematically usable (allowing that a few admit to "feeling shitty" about their decision to use the data). They have either shut out these emotions, or like the French woman in *Hiroshima mon amour*, they are not paying proper attention—they don't think to look around; they don't hear the endless cry.[54] They aren't motivated to seek genuine evaluative understanding, and so they altogether miss the data's true meaning. This results in harm—of the survivors and their descendants, the researchers, and our community.

Let us briefly pause to consider how researchers may be harmed by engaging the data, citing research on vicarious traumatization—a term coined by Lisa McCann and Laurie Anne Pearlman.[55] McCann and Pearlman explain that people who spend a significant portion of their professional time doing therapy with or studying persons who have been victimized experience "disruptions in their schemas about self and world."[56] For example, they may become suspicious of other people's motives, and more cynical, pessimistic, or distrustful. They may experience fearful thoughts or images associated with personal vulnerability, and they may take greater precautions against such a violation. They may experience a sense of alienation in their interpersonal relationships. They may experience flashbacks, dreams, or intrusive thoughts. Finally, they may feel sadness, anxiety, or anger.[57] Vicarious traumatization is not restricted to mental health professionals, but can also affect researchers and even educators.[58] Cynthia Lancaster et al. note that these PTSD-type symptoms can also develop "from repeated or extreme exposure to aversive details of traumatic events, such as military photographers whose job it is to photograph the details of wartime atrocities, first responders who are charged with collecting human remains, and police officers who are repeatedly exposed to details of childhood abuse."[59] Certainly poring over the horrific details of the victims' treatment in the Nazi's experiments, as researchers do, would count as repeated or extreme exposure to aversive details of traumatic events. To be sure, vicarious traumatization requires *empathic* engagement, as Pearlman and Karen W. Saakvitne,[60] among others, have noted.

If the survivors are right, then the researchers' (and medical ethicists') moral failure is inexcusable. They have justified what is unjustifiable. And they may not even recognize that they are doing this, especially given the long-standing stereotype of trauma survivors as emotional cripples. They need to critically reflect on and change their way of thinking, but this can prove all but impossible to do. As Goldie states, in such situations, "Doing this is not so easy, largely because of the possibility that one's epistemic landscape has *already* been skewed without one's knowing it . . . so one is not in a position, from the here and now of emotional experience, to take the dispassionate view of the evidence that the epistemic requirement demands."[61] And so the researchers become implicated in the evil perhaps without knowing it, perhaps without others knowing it (in particular, others who are also not paying proper attention).

Researchers, enmeshed in a culture that has historically stripped lives from "facts," have reinscribed the data just as the French have reinscribed Hiroshima (if we take *Hiroshima mon amour* to accurately reflect French culture). In both cases, this results in the effacement of death and a significant moral betrayal. In reinscribing the data's meaning from evil to a collection of anonymous "facts," in erasing the lives and experiences of past tortured selves, researchers commit a moral error, and one that rests on a cognitive error. Ultimately it is a failure of not paying proper attention, but they are no less blameworthy for it, even if they would have difficulty seeing their way out of it.

Consider the following example, presented by survivor Charlotte Delbo. At a Christmas party in Nazi Germany, a young German girl was given a little pink teddy bear with a ribbon around its neck. A Jewish girl left the teddy bear behind at the entrance to the "showers." A prisoner who worked in the crematoria found it among the objects piled up in the showers' antechamber and exchanged it for a couple of onions.[62] Michael Rothberg explains that a "chain of contamination" connects the murder of the Jewish girl with the celebration of the Christmas holiday. As he notes, the teddy bear was the carrier ("bearer" in his play on words) of a double heritage, and the fact that the narrator has accidentally seen the bear's original owner "ensures that the chain of evidence leading from murder to celebration will survive."[63]

While I do not want to suggest that little girls possess deep moral understanding, it seems right to suggest that once it is brought to the German girl's attention how the teddy bear was acquired, there is something morally wrong in her continuing to play with it. Similarly, once the real meaning of the data is brought to the researchers' attention (as it was at the 1989 conference), we should say that there is something morally wrong in their continuing to use it. But even if the girl never finds out about the teddy bear's origins, it seems that there is still something morally wrong with her playing with it. So too, even if the researchers' epistemic landscape has been so thoroughly skewed that they just cannot understand or accept the data's true meaning, there is still something wrong when they continue to use it. That is, their lack of knowledge is no excuse.

I can see four main objections to my account: (1) I make the notion of the self "meaningless" or "incoherent," since on this view the self "carries the whole world"; (2) If an object's meanings can be multifarious and conflicting, why should we privilege one meaning over the others (as I seem to be doing)?; (3) If the data is evil, and the survivors are the living data, then we arrive at the impossible conclusion that the survivors are evil; and perhaps most problematically, (4) while it makes sense to say that the victims are metaphorically present in the data, they are not literally present. Just as one is not actually aware of the presence of the former inhabitants of a ghost town, whom one knows, if at all, only by description and not by acquaintance, one is not actually aware of the presence of the victims when one interacts with the data. And there are similar worries about evil as contaminating. Evil is not literally a contaminant. Evil is not a thing. Let us consider each objection.

On a Merleau-Pontian account, when I interact with objects, I incorporate them into my self. That is, the self extends beyond the body container. In some cases, such as when I type on my laptop's keyboard, I literally incorporate the object into my bodily space; it becomes a part or extension of me. In all cases, when I interact with (cultural) objects, my body allows itself to be penetrated by new meanings; specifically, by meanings that the objects carry. When I interact with objects, I can also incorporate others' past experiences, especially when they are nested (as temporal objects) inside cultural objects, as the data is. My view seems to present a very "watered down" conception of the self, essentially making the self "meaningless" or "incoherent," since it seems to "carry the whole world"—or so the objection might go.

We can answer this objection by turning to Merleau-Ponty's notion of a "world horizon," which I briefly articulated above. In a sense it is true that I carry the whole world, but in nowise does this make the self "meaningless" or "incoherent." This is an unavoidable consequence of living in a deeply social world thoroughly imbued with meaning. Although I carry the whole world, most of the parts remain implicitly present—indeterminate, ambiguous, remote, and hidden—unless I pay attention. As Merleau-Ponty explains, "I apply my gaze to a fragment of the landscape, which becomes animated and displayed, while the other objects recede into the margins and become dormant, *but they do not cease to be there*."[64]

The horizon also includes the implicit presentation of past (and future) stages of temporal objects. That is, similar to the perceptual horizon (of objects in space), retentions and protentions are part of the structure of my current experience. So I do carry the whole world, but most of it is remote and ambiguous. Parts of it will be more determinate and proximate—specifically those objects to which I pay attention. These (cultural/temporal) objects will be presented explicitly, while the rest of the horizon will be part of the background, and may only vaguely present themselves.

But for those who may feel a bit "unsettled" about this conception of the self, perhaps we do not need to make it this "extensive" to adequately capture the victims' relationship to the data. Perhaps we can merely say that the data falls within the boundaries of their selves by *representing* their lived experiences. Of course there is a lot of Holocaust material (literature, art, film, photographs, and so on), which represents the victims' harms, and yet we do not always presume that the victims have anything like ownership claims over it. We need, then, a principled way of determining why some physical representations falling within the boundaries of the self count with respect to ownership (and thus with claims to control) while others do not. It is not altogether unreasonable, for example, to argue that the photos of ghetto camp inmates displayed on the walls of a museum ought to be given to the photographed persons or their families should they request them. It seems far less reasonable to suggest that the thousands of Jews who were saved by the villagers of Le Chambon should receive royalties from books written about them.

So what is the difference here? Might it be the level of intimacy in the representation? A photograph can be one of the most intimate exposures of a person, possibly leaving the person tremendously vulnerable. If a person snaps a photo of me on the street, should I have a right to that photo? What if it were displayed in a public gallery? Recent lawsuits were unsuccessfully brought against artist/photographer, Arne Svenson, who secretly photographed his neighbors' intimate moments in an adjacent New York high rise without getting their permission, and then displayed them in national art exhibits. Art critic Ray Mark Rinaldi called Svenson's controversial exhibit, entitled "The Neighbors," "deeply offensive," describing Svenson's actions as "not a victimless crime."[65] Rinaldi was not alone among art critics in his assessment. Does it matter *how* I am represented? It seems so. If I am represented in a vulnerable way, or one that betrays my (moral) character, then it seems that I should have a right to that photograph.

In "the naked truth," Arthur Danto argues that people have the right to control how they are represented. In controlling the telling of my experiences, I control how I am represented. Being denied that control is a violation of my right. While one may not think that the data intimately represents the victims' lives (although I suggest that it might be one of the most intimate representations, displaying violations of bodily integrity), the survivors (or their families) want to control how they wish to be seen and regarded.

Danto concerns himself with "the rights of individuals over the way they appear."[66] He tells us about an exhibition at the Art Institute of Chicago, in which someone displayed a painting of former Chicago mayor Harold Washington wearing nothing but frilly women's underwear. Even though Washington was dead at the time, the painting violated Washington's right to correct representation. Danto explains that "it was an exceedingly cruel painting, implying secret vices on the mayor's part or suggesting a metaphor for which there was no obvious interpretation that corresponded to any known fact of the mayor's character or behavior."[67] Analogously, when we use the data (especially if we understand it as falling within the boundaries of the victims' selves) we are in danger of depicting the victims as no more than "useful" information or things.

The Nazis have already painted an exceedingly humiliating picture of their victims. When we maintain control over the data (and more specifically, when we use it), we agree with the Nazis that their victims were no more than useful things. When we control the data, we continue to fill in the picture in this way, taking over where the Nazis left off. Or if we want to think of the painting as already complete, we allow the Nazis' painting to remain displayed, hanging in the gallery of our world. But if we give the survivors control, the picture changes. The survivors (or if they are deceased, their families or their community) paint a new picture, showing the Nazis, themselves, and the world that they are autonomous agents capable of making moral decisions of lasting importance. We also proclaim to the world that they are not things. In this way, the survivors can finish telling the stories of their experiences. Getting a say-so about the data's use constitutes the "final chapter," so to speak, in the narrative of their traumatic experiences as experimental "subjects." But so long as we maintain control of the data (using it; deciding what should be done with it), *we* control their story.

But is the data more like a painting or more like a photograph? Kendall Walton argues that when we look at a photograph, we *actually see* the person who was photographed, just as we actually see the person we are looking at through our binoculars. The photographed person is *really present* in the photo, just as the victims are *really present* in the data. *We see them.* Walton cites André Bazin's "The Ontology of the Photographic Image," in which Bazin writes that the photographic image is the object itself.[68] Walton appeals to our intuitions about photographed people, noting that

> Some courts allow reporters to sketch their proceedings but not to photograph them. Photographs are more useful for extortion; a sketch of Mr. X with Mrs. Y—even a full color oil painting—would cause little consternation. Photographic pornography is more potent than the painted variety. Published photographs of disaster victims or the private lives of public figures understandably provoke charges of invasion of privacy; similar complaints against the publication of drawings and painting have less credibility.[69]

As Walton explains, with the assistance of the camera, we not only see what is distant or small, for example, but we can also *see into the past*: "We see long deceased ancestors when we look at dusty snapshots of them. . . . Photographs are *transparent.* We see the world *through* them."[70]

Walton warns against a "watered down" version of his view. He states quite emphatically: "My claim is that we see, *quite literally*, our dead relatives themselves when we look at photographs of them."[71] To be sure, we see the photographed people or objects *indirectly*; however, perception is equally indirect in many other cases as well. By contrast, paintings are not like this. They are not transparent: "We do not see Henry VIII when we look at his portrait; we see only a representation of him."[72]

Despite possible misgivings about a conception of the self in which the data is *literally* a part of the victims' selves, or that we *literally* see or experience the victims *in the data*, Walton's insights support my claim for this stronger interpretation: the victims' experiences are not merely represented in the data, the victims *themselves* are present in it, and so when we interact with the data, we *literally experience the victims*, albeit indirectly.

But is Walton's transparency thesis any good? Walton has been accused, by Nigel Warburton (1988), Jonathan Friday (1996), and others, of using a slippery slope argument to support his thesis, moving from uncontroversial cases of seeing through certain instruments, such as eyeglasses, mirrors, telescopes, and binoculars, to the controversial case of photographic transparency. Slippery slope arguments are notoriously unreliable. Warburton, for example, has identified a "cluster of features" to the concept of seeing, which provides theoretical differences sufficient to halt the slide to photographic transparency (namely, virtual simultaneity, temporal congruity, sensitivity to change, and knowledge of the causal chain).

Walton's transparency thesis is still helpful in our case, at least insofar as it contributes to our understanding of how victims can be present in the data, and how we come to see them. However, victims "present themselves" differently from the ordinary way we see people through binoculars or a camera lens. Recall that on a Merleau-Pontian account, we can become aware of other selves as subjects or objects. When I am aware of someone as an object, my experience of that person is on a par with my awareness of things such as cars and coffee cups. When we interact with the Nazi data, we literally experience the victims, but we "see them" in a different manner. We don't see them as if looking at them through binoculars or a camera lens. We see them more in the manner that we "see" someone when viewing their MRI scan.

Settling on the view that the victims are merely metaphorically in the data, or that the data merely represents their experiences, does not adequately capture survivors' claims that they are the living data of the Nazi experiments and that when we use the data we use them, and it is this latter, stronger sense of presence that we need—especially if I am correct that the survivors have a deeper understanding of the self's relationship to the world and do not merely mean to call attention to the data's savage history. The best approach, if we are going to take seriously the survivors' words as accurately depicting their experiences, is to hold firm to a Merleau-Pontian conception of the self and its relationship to cultural/temporal objects.

The second objection concerns privileging one meaning over other multifarious and sometimes conflicting meanings. Am I entitled to privilege one meaning over others especially when, as Merleau-Ponty suggests, neither meanings nor even the past are "fixed"? To answer this, it seems that even if I have "altered" the past (it is not the past itself, but the past such as I now remember it) or have reinscribed meanings of certain objects and events (such as Hiroshima, or the teddy bear, or the Nazi data), the object/event "beckons" me to respond to its "true" meaning *when I pay proper attention*. If so, we should privilege that true meaning. It may be up for discussion how we should then *respond* to that meaning, whether we should respond in the way that it invites us to respond. But if we follow Coetzee's *Elizabeth Costello*, at least in our case there is only one appropriate response. Costello talks about the cellar in which the July 1944 plotters were hanged: "I believe that bars should be erected over the cellar mouth, with a bronze memorial plaque saying *Here died* . . . followed by a list of the dead and their dates, and that should be that."[73] Survivors in our debate have made similar claims. Recall that one survivor remarked that if *she* had control of the data, she would shred it and put it into "a glass monument with the inscription underneath, 'No human guinea pigs again.'"

This objection invites a discussion about the politics of meaning inscription. To understand this, let us look briefly at Shannon Sullivan's charge that Merleau-Ponty's phenomenology presents a model of domination. While many people, for example Stoller (2000) and Weiss (2002), have successfully defended Merleau-Ponty against Sullivan's charge, it is nonetheless instructive to bring her in here. Sullivan calls Merleau-Ponty's project a phenomenology of "projective intentionality," in which I "impose" meanings on others: I "impose my way of understanding and taking up my world on another and thus fail to realize that others may take up their worlds differently."[74]

Merleau-Ponty does in fact highlight difference. Let us consider his words:

> The other's grief or anger never has precisely the same sense for him and for me. For him, these are lived situations; for me, they are appresented. Or if I can participate in this grief or in this anger through a gesture of friendship, they remain the grief and the anger of my friend Paul: he suffers because he has lost his wife, or he is angry because his watch has been stolen; I suffer because Paul is grieving or I am angry because he is angry—the two situations are not congruent. And finally, if we undertake a shared project, this shared project is not a single project, and it is not presented to me and to Paul from the same angle; we are not equally committed to it, or at least not committed to it in the same way, from the mere fact that Paul is Paul, and I am myself.[75]

Despite Sullivan seemingly having gotten this point wrong about Merleau-Ponty's phenomenology, it is nonetheless helpful to look at her proposed alternative—what she calls "hypothetical construction." As she puts it, "Hypothetical construction . . . suggests a way that my world takes on meaning with and through others because meaning is seen as a construction: a building-together of meaning through debate, conflict, negotiation, disagreement, and agreement . . . my hypothesis (that is, the meaning I initially give the encounter) is offered, not projected."[76] In this way, my meaning is presented as an invitation, which can be accepted, rejected, revised, or supplemented as part of the negotiation of meaning.

As we will see in the final chapter, people in positions of power, people who do not always take their interlocutors to be epistemically credible, often impose meanings on objects or events and assume or insist that their interlocutors share these same meaning inscriptions. Given this, Sullivan's proposed "hypothetical construction" seems like a good solution to problems of this type, in that those who are considered to be less epistemically credible can have a voice in the debate, and more to the point: a voice that will be taken *seriously*. I will argue that, despite the so-called experts in our debate claiming otherwise, the survivors are the *real moral experts* (they are correct in saying so), and so we should listen to them. Of course experts are by no means infallible. However, if survivors are indeed the experts, then we should pay serious attention to what they say. I allow that some survivors may have distorted judgments due to their trauma. But if the preponderance of testimony presents a particular point of view, we should be inclined to accept it.

Let us briefly address the concern about transitivity: if the data is evil, and survivors are the living data, then it seems to follow that the survivors are evil. But we certainly do not want to say that. I argue that this relationship is not transitive, invoking what I call a "chicken gumbo" analogy. It goes like this: Chicken is necessary for chicken gumbo. Chicken gumbo is spicy, but of course the chicken itself is not spicy. So too, the survivors are a necessary part of the Nazi data (the data would not be evil, were it not for the victims' experiences); however, although the data is evil, the survivors are not.

Finally, let us consider the objection that evil is not literally a contaminant. When the survivors claim that the data is literally evil, this suggests some kind of (magical, mysterious) "metaphysical taint." We can certainly make sense of their claim that the data is metaphorically or symbolically evil, but it is not literally evil—or so the objection goes. I suggest a way that the Nazi data is a *real* moral contagion. When we use the data we *literally* implicate ourselves in the evil.

The move is to understand evil as a *property* of a thing, rather than a thing. Evil is a *contaminating property* that implicates us in evil—evil as understood in the sense Card describes. There are things that are evil (just as there are things that are red or smelly, and so on), but evil is not a thing. Certain plants—hemlock of course, or rhubarb leaves—cause violent, painful convulsions, and death when ingested. Poison ivy or poison oak causes itching, irritating, and sometimes painful rash in most people who touch it. Analogously, the Nazi data is a moral contagion: we become morally tainted when we use it, implicated in the evil of the experiments. Similar arguments can be made for (knowingly) using "dirty" money, wearing sweatshop garments, and consuming meat from factory farming, or donning fur coats. We are now ready to consider a final reason that survivors give for controlling the data: because they are the moral experts in the debate and they know what best to do with it. I do this in the final chapter, after first explaining how calling survivors emotional cripples counts as a further harm and thus works against their healing.

NOTES

1. Maurice Merleau-Ponty, *Phenomenology of Perception*, trans. Donald A. Landes (New York: Routledge, 2012), 456.
2. Peter Goldie, "Emotion, Reason, and Virtue," in *Emotion, Evolution, and Rationality*, eds. Dylan Evans and Pierre Cruse (Oxford University Press, 2004), 255.
3. *Ibid.*, 249, 256.

4. Cathy Caruth, *Unclaimed Experience: Trauma, Narrative, and History* (Baltimore: Johns Hopkins University Press, 1996), 29.

5. Maurice Merleau-Ponty, *Phenomenology of Perception*, trans. Donald A. Landes (New York: Routledge, 2012), 379.

6. *Ibid.*, 331.

7. *Ibid.*, 335–36.

8. *Ibid.*, 146.

9. *Ibid.*, 148.

10. See Shannon Sullivan, "Domination and Dialogue in Merleau-Ponty's Phenomenology of Perception," *Hypatia* 12, no. 1 (1997).

11. *Ibid.*, 145–46.

12. *Ibid.*, 154.

13. *Ibid.*, 146.

14. *Ibid.*, 363.

15. Komarine Romdenh-Romluc, *Routledge Philosophy Guidebook to Merleau-Ponty and Phenomenology of Perception* (New York: Routledge, 2011), 135.

16. *Ibid.*, 135–36.

17. Claudia Card, *The Atrocity Paradigm: A Theory of Evil* (Oxford: Oxford University Press, 2002), 3–4.

18. J. M. Coetzee, *Elizabeth Costello* (New York: Penguin Books, 2003), 173.

19. *Ibid.*, 175.

20. *Ibid.*, 176, my emphasis.

21. Nicolle Jordan, "A Creole Contagion: Narratives of Slavery and Tainted Wealth in *Millennium Hall*," *Tulsa Studies in Women's Literature* 30, no. 1 (2011): 57–58.

22. Komarine Romdenh-Romluc, *Routledge Philosophy Guidebook to Merleau-Ponty and Phenomenology of Perception* (New York: Routledge, 2011), 125–26.

23. *Ibid.*, 246–47.

24. Maurice Merleau-Ponty, *Phenomenology of Perception*, trans. Donald A. Landes (New York: Routledge, 2012), 71.

25. *Ibid.*, 434, my emphasis.

26. *Ibid.*, 71–72.

27. Komarine Romdenh-Romluc, *Routledge Philosophy Guidebook to Merleau-Ponty and Phenomenology of Perception* (New York: Routledge, 2011), 234.

28. Maurice Merleau-Ponty, *Phenomenology of Perception*, trans. Donald A. Landes (New York: Routledge, 2012), 141.

29. Komarine Romdenh-Romluc, *Routledge Philosophy Guidebook to Merleau-Ponty and Phenomenology of Perception* (New York: Routledge, 2011), 231.

30. *Ibid.*

31. Dori Laub, "Bearing Witness, or the Vicissitudes of Listening," in *Testimony: Crises of Witnessing in Literature, Psychoanalysis, and History*, eds. Shoshana Felman and Dori Laub (New York: Routledge, 1992), 69.

32. Marianne Hirsch, "Marked by Memory: Feminist Reflections on Trauma and Transmission," in *Extremities: Trauma, Testimony, and Community*, eds. Nancy K. Miller and Jason Tougaw (Champaign: University of Illinois Press, 2002), 71.

33. *Ibid.*, 73.

34. Maurice Merleau-Ponty, *Phenomenology of Perception*, trans. Donald A. Landes (New York: Routledge, 2012), 457, my emphasis.

35. Iris Murdoch, *The Italian Girl* (New York: Vintage, 2000), 68, my emphasis.

36. Marianne Hirsch, "Marked by Memory: Feminist Reflections on Trauma and Transmission," in *Extremities: Trauma, Testimony, and Community*, eds. Nancy K. Miller and Jason Tougaw (Champaign: University of Illinois Press, 2002), 75.

37. *Ibid.*

38. Mallory E. Bowers and Rachel Yehuda, "Intergenerational Transmission of Stress in Humans," *Neuropsychopharmacology REVIEWS* 41 (2016): 235.

39. See Rachel Yehuda et al., "Relationship Between Posttraumatic Stress Disorder Characteristics of Holocaust Survivors and their Adult Offspring," *The American Journal of Psychiatry* 155, no. 6 (June 1998): 841–43.

40. *Ibid.*, 233.

41. *Ibid.*, 232–44. See also R. Yehuda and L. M. Bierer, "The Relevance of Epigenetics to PTSD: Implications for the DSM-V," *Journal of Trauma Stress* 22 (2009): 427–34; and R. Yehuda et al., "Influences of Maternal and Paternal PTSD on Epigenetic Regulation of the Glucocorticoid Receptor Gene in Holocaust Survivor Offspring," *American Journal of Psychiatry* 171 (2014): 872–80.

42. Miri Scharf, "Long-term Effects of Trauma: Psychosocial Functioning of the Second and Third Generation of Holocaust Survivors," *Development and Psychopathology* 19 (2007): 603–22.

43. Peter Goldie, "Emotion, Reason, and Virtue," in *Emotion, Evolution, and Rationality*, eds. Dylan Evans and Pierre Cruse (Oxford: Oxford University Press, 2004), 255.

44. P. Vuilleumier, J. Armony, and R. Dolan, "Reciprocal Links Between Emotion and Attention," in *Human Brain Function*, 2nd edition, eds. R. S. J. Frackowiak et al. (San Diego: Academic Press, 2003).

45. *Ibid.*, 253.

46. Michael Brady, *Emotional Insight: The Epistemic Role of Emotional Experience* (Oxford: Oxford University Press, 2013), 180.

47. Martha Nussbaum, *Love's Knowledge* (Oxford: Oxford University Press), 70.

48. Peter Goldie, "Emotion, Reason, and Virtue," in *Emotion, Evolution, and Rationality*, eds. Dylan Evans and Pierre Cruse (Oxford: Oxford University Press, 2004), 260.

49. Michael Brady, *Emotional Insight: The Epistemic Role of Emotional Experience* (Oxford: Oxford University Press, 2013), 174.

50. Michael Brady, "Emotions, Perceptions, and Reasons," in *Morality and the Emotions*, ed. Carla Bagnoli (Oxford: Oxford University Press, 2011), 142.

51. Michael Brady, *Emotional Insight: The Epistemic Role of Emotional Experience* (Oxford: Oxford University Press, 2013), 176.

52. Cathy Caruth, *Unclaimed Experience: Trauma, Narrative, and History* (Baltimore: Johns Hopkins University Press, 1996), 25–26.

53. *Ibid.*, 29.

54. *Ibid.*, Note 4, 122.

55. Lisa McCann and Laurie Anne Pearlman, "Vicarious Traumatization: A Framework for Understanding the Psychological Effects of Working with Victims," *Journal of Traumatic Stress* 3, no. 1 (1990): 131–49.

56. *Ibid.*, 138. See also Laurie Anne Pearlman and Karen W. Saakvitne, "Treating Therapists with Vicarious Traumatization and Secondary Traumatic Stress Disorders," in *Compassion Fatigue: Coping with Secondary Traumatic Stress Disorder in Those Who Treat the Traumatized*, ed. Charles R. Figley (New York: Routledge, 2015), 150–77.

57. *Ibid.*, 138–41.

58. See, for example, Beth Hudnall Stamm, ed. *Secondary Traumatic Stress: Self-Care Issues for Clinicians, Researchers, and Educators* (Brooklandville, MD: Sidran Institute Press, 1999).

59. Cynthia Lancaster et al., "Posttraumatic Stress Disorder: Overview of Evidence Based Assessment and Treatment," *Journal of Clinical Medicine* 5, no. 11 (November 2016).

60. Laurie Anne Pearlman and Karen W. Saakvitne, *Trauma and the Therapist: Countertransference and Vicarious Traumatization in Psychotherapy with Incest Survivors* (New York: W. W. Norton and Company, 1995).

61. Peter Goldie, "Emotion, Reason, and Virtue," in *Emotion, Evolution, and Rationality*, eds. Dylan Evans and Pierre Cruse (Oxford: Oxford University Press, 2004), 260.

62. Charlotte Delbo, *Auschwitz and After*, 2nd edition, trans. Rosette C. Lamont (New Haven, CT: Yale University Press, 2014), 166.

63. Michael Rothberg, "Between the Extreme and the Everyday: Ruth Klüger's Traumatic Realism," in *Extremities: Trauma, Testimony, and Community*, eds. Nancy K. Miller and Jason Tougaw (Champaign: University of Illinois, 2002), 61–62.

64. Maurice Merleau-Ponty, *Phenomenology of Perception*, trans. Donald A. Landes (New York: Routledge, 2012), 70, my emphasis.

65. See Stephanie Wolf, "Art, or Invasion of Privacy: Photographer Arne Svenson's MCA Exhibit Raises Eyebrows," *Colorado Public Radio* at cpr.org. May 27, 2016.

66. Arthur Danto, "the naked truth," in *Aesthetics and Ethics: Essays at the Intersection (Cambridge Studies in Philosophy and the Arts)*, revised edition, ed. Jerrold Levinson (Cambridge: Cambridge University Press, 2001), 267.

67. *Ibid.*, 267–68.

68. Kendall Walton, "Transparent Pictures: On the Nature of Photographic Realism," *Critical Inquiry* 11, no. 2 (1984): 246.

69. *Ibid.*, 247.

70. *Ibid.*, 251.

71. *Ibid.*, 252.

72. *Ibid.*, 253.

73. J. M. Coetzee, *Elizabeth Costello* (New York: Penguin Books, 2003), 173.

74. Shannon Sullivan, "Domination and Dialogue in Merleau-Ponty's Phenomenology of Perception," *Hypatia* 12, no. 1 (1997): 8.

75. Maurice Merleau-Ponty, *Phenomenology of Perception*, trans. Donald A. Landes (New York: Routledge, 2012), 372.

76. Shannon Sullivan, "Domination and Dialogue in Merleau-Ponty's Phenomenology of Perception," *Hypatia* 12, no. 1 (1997): 10.

Chapter 6

Epistemic Injustice and the Survivors' Claims to Moral Expertise

The so-called experts (researchers and medical ethicists) have controlled what counts as legitimate knowledge claims in our debate. Only those claims that are "rational," "objective," accessible to all, and have the capacity to be verified or falsified, are taken seriously, and they consign to "epistemic limbo" those who profess "crazy, bizarre, or outlandish beliefs."[1] Of course since the so-called experts have all of the power in our debate, they decide what counts as crazy, bizarre, and outlandish in the first place.

Thus far, I have argued that the Nazi data should be given to the survivors, not because they are experts, but because the data belongs to them, and doing so would help restore their dignity/*kavod* and thus work toward their healing. In this final chapter, I discuss a further reason we should give survivors control of the data, namely, because they are the real moral experts in the debate, as they argue. One reason to spend time motivating this claim is that survivors explicitly state that the data is evil and we continue to harm them, the community, and ourselves when we use it. This insight, they state, is grounded in their experience. That is, they claim that their experience puts them in an epistemic advantage in our debate. Clearly, to bestow moral expertise on the survivors is to dignify them. So if we decide to defer to the survivors in this way, not only do we help them heal in ways previously articulated, but we further dignify them by bestowing this important honor.

I proceed as follows. First, I discuss how the survivors' treatment in our debate is incontrovertibly an instance of what Miranda Fricker and others call "epistemic injustice." Next, I explain that even though those who command epistemic authority experience many epistemic advantages at the expense of less privileged members of an epistemic community, these more marginalized and excluded members can also experience epistemic advantages of their own, in virtue of their position vis-à-vis the more advantaged members, which gives them what José Medina, following W. E. B. Du Bois, calls a "double consciousness." In discussing this, I draw on insights from standpoint epistemology. Further, I discuss the value of knowledge by testimony and trusting others' (moral) expertise, since the survivors' claims are grounded in testimony. I argue, against pessimists who reject moral testimony and moral expertise, that we should trust the survivors' testimony because they satisfy all of the criteria for moral expertise. Finally, I argue that we should show the survivors what Laurence Thomas calls "moral deference," especially since (1) they are the real moral experts in our debate; (2) we have never taken them seriously; (3) they have already suffered a triple indignity; and (4) we can work toward repairing harm by doing what they say.

An epistemic injustice occurs when a speaker who is on the receiving end of the injustice is harmed in her capacity as a knower, because her claims are discredited as so much nonsense. Often she is discredited to such an extent that the audience misses out on knowledge of indispensable value. This is certainly true in our debate, as I have argued. As Fricker notes, this results in a profound harm, and not merely an epistemic harm. This undermines the speaker's very humanity, and if the discrediting is done before an audience as it was in the 1989 conference (and at other venues, including my Haifa talk), this is profoundly humiliating.

Far from being "emotional cripples," the survivors are right when they claim to be the *real* experts in this debate. In virtue of their experiences, they know what is really going on, what matters, and what meanings, values, and questions we should attend to. Despite what some of the "experts" say in our debate, the survivors are in fact in an epistemically advantageous position knowing things that are inaccessible to those who have not had their experiences. However, since "cool rationality" runs the debate, the so-called experts (who take themselves to be the epistemically credible ones, since they have the accepted credentials and appropriate "pedigrees") cannot make sense of what the survivors are trying to say, and so they dismiss them from a position of epistemic arrogance.

While experience does not grant a person automatic epistemic privilege, I argue that given the relevance of the survivors' experiences to our debate as just the sort of experience required for moral understanding, they are clearly the moral experts. Recall that in the 1989 conference, an audience member called a survivor an "emotional cripple," "ruled by emotions and not by the mind," and therefore unqualified to participate in the debate. Since the survivor's claims did not exhibit "cool rationality," they were dismissed as the rants of an emotional cripple tied to the horrors of the past. This is a clear case of what Fricker, Medina, and others call "epistemic injustice." Such injustices have been prevalent throughout our debate and constitute profound harms.

As Mira Giberovitch explains, calling the survivor an "emotional cripple" negatively affects both her and her community. The survivor often internalizes this judgment within her self-concept and then transmits it to second- and third-generation offspring. The person who accepts these negative images of herself loses self-esteem and this undermines her dignity/*kavod*. Giberovitch shares a story of a survivor—a former teacher who with tears in her eyes shares the self-doubt that she has lived with for many years. Although she was an educator within the Jewish community, she felt stigmatized as a Holocaust survivor. After reading the clinical literature, she doubted her own capabilities as a parent and teacher.[2]

We will focus on a special case of what Fricker calls "testimonial injustice": when prejudice causes a hearer to *deflate* the credibility of a speaker's words. By associating trauma victims with emotional cripples, the audience member (and other participants in our debate) deflates the credibility of the survivor's words to such an extent that he (and, indeed, the conference participants and larger research and medical ethics communities) misses out on the knowledge articulated in the previous chapters.

Such communicative exchanges which result in epistemic injustices are "a normal part of discursive life."[3] That is, we wrongly assume that epistemic injustice is an aberration of discourse. This is because epistemic practices are always socially situated, in which people stand in differing relationships of power with each other. Epistemic injustice can be found everywhere, often without our awareness, and can be extraordinarily subtle. Laurence Thomas explains,

> It can be assumed, for example, often without awareness of what is being done, that this or that category of person cannot measure up in an important way. That we do not expect much of a person on account of her social category can be communicated in a thousand and one ways. One may listen inattentively, or interrupt frequently, or not directly respond to what the person actually says, or not respond with the seriousness that is appropriate to the person concerned.[4]

Fricker introduces the notion of testimonial injustice by discussing Anthony Minghella's screenplay of *The Talented Mr. Ripley*. Herbert Greenleaf responds to his future daughter-in-law Marge's suspicion that Tom Ripley, a supposed friend of Greenleaf's son Dickie, is in fact Dickie's murderer. As Fricker notes, Greenleaf uses a familiar sexist put down to silence Marge: "Marge, there's female intuition, and then there are facts." Greenleaf's silencing of Marge involves an exercise of power, and of gender power in particular. Gender power is a type of identity power, which depends upon agents "having shared conceptions of social identity—conceptions alive in the collective social imagination that govern, for instance, what it means to be a woman or a man, or what it means to be gay or straight, young or old, and so on."[5] In the case of Herbert Greenleaf, Fricker notes that he is "ingenuously trying to persuade Marge to take what he regards as a more objective view of the situation, a situation which he correctly sees as highly stressful and emotionally charged for her."[6] Further, Greenleaf might not even be aware that he is using gendered stereotypes to silence Marge, and indeed he might even be well-intentioned and paternal. It turns out, of course, that Marge is right about her "intuition," but Greenleaf's prejudice causes him to miss out on this important piece of knowledge.

The interaction between the audience member and the survivor in our debate is strikingly similar to the interaction between Greenleaf and Marge. In our debate, the audience member exercises power by drawing on a familiar stereotype of the trauma victim as an "emotional cripple." In our debate, the audience member takes what he regards as the more objective view of the exchange, an exchange that he correctly sees as highly stressful and emotionally charged for the survivor (and of course rightly so). In our debate, though it seems difficult to imagine, it might be that the audience member was not even aware that he was exercising power in this way. And as I argue, it turns out that in our case the survivor (like Marge) is right, but the audience member and other participants in the debate miss out on knowledge of indispensable value, because their prejudice blinds them.

What is this knowledge? As we have seen: (1) using the data without the survivors' consent harms them, it harms their dignity/*kavod*; (2) since they are the "living data" of the experiments, they alone should control the data (they should decide what should be done with it); (3) they are the real (moral) experts in the debate, in virtue of their experiences (not the researchers and medical ethicists, despite their "credentials"); and (4) the Nazi data is evil (*really* evil, not merely symbolically evil), and we become morally tainted when we use it.

Fricker explains that such examples of identity prejudice, such as we have in our debate, are often at work in stereotypes. As she notes, many of the stereotypes of historically powerless and marginalized groups involve attributions of epistemic incompetence or insincerity, including over-emotionality, illogicality, or inferior intelligence. The marginalized speaker is given little, if any, epistemic credibility. Indeed, sometimes her credibility is already considered to be so deficient that her testimony is not even solicited. That is, she is literally passed over in silence. As a result, the marginalized speaker is wrongfully excluded from the community of epistemically credible subjects of knowledge, of epistemic agents.

Medina notes that, oftentimes, marginalized groups are not excluded in communicative exchanges altogether, but even so:

Members of different groups may enjoy quite different voices . . . and they may be heard differently. In other words, even when people are not entirely excluded from participation, their communicative agency may be constrained or compromised in important ways; and the appreciation of their contributions may not be on a par with that of others.[7]

This is clearly at work in our debate. Although some survivors spoke at the conference, they were taken to be overly emotional, and their contributions were not taken seriously. As Medina explains, in communicative contexts, which are typically populated by differently situated voices with differing epistemic agency, varying groups are often treated as subjects of knowledge "but without the full range of epistemic capacities that other subjects enjoy."[8] Further, in some situations, the speaker has "next to no chance of getting herself understood when she is struggling to make sense of something . . . *because her interlocutors have been trained not to hear or to hear only deficiently and through a lens that filters out the speaker's perspective.*"[9] This is an example of what Fricker calls "hermeneutical injustice," which occurs when the speaker is unable to "properly" articulate herself within the "dominant" discourse. Medina notes that under such circumstances, most hearers display little interpretive charity.

We can see this at work in our debate. Since their communicative style tends to be one of "cool rationality," most participants (the researchers and medical ethicists) cannot make sense of what the survivors are trying to communicate. Instead, they hear only deficiently, because they have been trained to filter out—to dismiss as irrational—emotionally charged epistemic claims. Further, since survivors do not speak the so-called experts' language, they do not articulate themselves in the "proper" manner, and so they struggle to make themselves understood. Even more so, because the "experts" are confronted with traumatic testimony, they use defensive strategies to try to insulate themselves from what is being said, to protect themselves, as Dori Laub puts it, "from the offshoots of the trauma and from the intensity of the flood of affect that, through the testimony, comes to be directed toward [them]."[10] As a result, not only do we harm the survivors in all of the ways that I have articulated above, we introduce yet another serious harm in our dismissal of their claims and our decision to continue to use the data despite their protests: we undermine their humanity, and we degrade and humiliate them. Let me explain what I mean.

Fricker notes that there is a purely epistemic harm whenever a prejudicial stereotype deflates epistemic credibility: the knowledge that would have been passed on to a hearer is not received.[11] As a result, the testimonial injustice "damages the epistemic system." But there is a far more egregious harm, and not merely an epistemic harm, that the hearer does to the speaker who is the victim of this type of injustice. When a person is wronged in her capacity as a knower, she is wronged in a capacity that is essential to human value. As Fricker explains, "the capacity to give knowledge to others is one side of the many-sided capacity so significant in human beings; namely, the capacity for reason." She notes that it is precisely our rationality that lends humanity its distinctive value.[12] And so when we wrong a person in this way, we undermine her very humanity. The epistemic wrong "bears a social *meaning* to the effect that the subject is less than fully human." The person is degraded "*qua* knower and symbolically degraded *qua* human." And such a dehumanizing meaning, especially when expressed before others, can be profoundly humiliating.[13] In the survivors' case, this constitutes a further indignity.

Medina notes that while the socio-politically and economically advantaged enjoy many epistemic benefits, such as access to information, access to educational institutions, capacity to disseminate knowledge and to command epistemic authority, the less privileged members, while certainly experiencing epistemic disadvantages (including being marginalized in or excluded from epistemic practices) can also experience epistemic advantages.[14] This is an important lesson of feminist standpoint epistemology.

Beginning around the 1970s, feminists started paying attention to the relationship between the production of knowledge and the exercise of power. Feminist standpoint theory was born out of these efforts as both an epistemology and a methodology—a prescriptive method for understanding, criticizing, and "doing" epistemology.[15] We can trace standpoint theory's roots back to the literary tradition of realism, popular in the United States, England, and parts of Europe, which began around the 1830s and maintained its popularity until the end of that century. Realism rejects overly romantic and exaggerated narratives, and instead favors the everyday experiences of everyday people, including the historically marginalized.

Authors, such as Mark Twain, Kate Chopin, Hamlin Garland, Charlotte Perkins Gilman, and Du Bois depict experiences different from the mainstream and reveal the value of these experiences. In *The Souls of Black Folk*, Du Bois anticipates, by about eighty years, what standpoint theorists such as Uma Narayan call "double vision," in which "the oppressed are seen as having an 'epistemic advantage' because they can operate with two sets of practices and in two different contexts. This advantage is thought to lead to critical insights because each framework provides a critical perspective on the other."[16]

According to traditional, "modernist" epistemological approaches, the best epistemic standpoint is one of a neutral, disinterested observer, abstracted from all history and sociopolitical life, who holds a "view from nowhere," or a "God's eye view." This standpoint was presumed to produce the most impartial, comprehensive, value-free, and "objective" knowledge. But as standpoint theorists such as Sandra Harding were quick to point out, there is no such standpoint. Rather, so-called "objective" knowledge claims are merely the claims of the privileged, "epistemically competent" members of a community—claims that reflect, privilege, and protect *their* social values and interests, and eliminate those different from their own.[17] Far from being disinterested and objective, this standpoint actually reflects the privileged (dominant) group's racist, sexist, classist, heterosexist, etc., beliefs. The privileged group controls the production of knowledge and insulates its members from those who are disadvantaged, marginalized, or oppressed, leading them to believe that their perspective, the one that justifies their interpretation of reality, is the correct one—indeed, the only one.[18]

Standpoint theorists recognize that social location (and in particular, one's position vis-à-vis differing power relations) shapes and limits what we know. Knowledge is always, as they say, "situated."[19] Further, standpoint theorists argue that a good epistemic starting point is from the perspective of marginalized lives. As Harding recognizes, this will often generate illuminating critical questions that do not arise from within the dominant group.[20] The result will be more impartial, less distorted, more comprehensive, and more "objective," because it introduces multiple, heterogeneous, often contradictory perspectives rather than narrowly reflecting the privileged group's perspective.

Another theme of standpoint epistemology is its recognition of the importance of emotion and value in the construction of knowledge. As Narayan notes, standpoint theory "has tried to reintegrate values and emotions into our account of our cognitive activities, arguing for both the inevitability of their presence and the importance of the contributions they are capable of making to our knowledge. It has also attacked various sets of dualisms characteristic of western philosophical thinking," including reason/emotion.[21]

The standpoint of the socio-politically or economically marginalized or oppressed is not just different, but potentially epistemically advantageous, often challenging the perspective of the dominant group. As Harding explains,

> Everywhere, seemingly every day, another under-advantaged group steps on the stage of history and says "from the standpoint of our lives, what you over-advantaged people think and do looks different . . . and wrong and harmful." It is the "wrong and harmful" that is morally and intellectually the most disturbing force of standpoint thinking because this judgment challenges the presumed reasonableness and progressiveness of dominant institutional assumptions and practices.[22]

Alison Wylie calls this the "inversion thesis." As she describes it,

> Those who are subject to structures of domination that systematically marginalize and oppress them may, in fact, be epistemically privileged in some crucial

respects. They may know different things, or know things better than those who are comparatively privileged (socially, politically), by virtue of what they typically experience and how they understand their experience.[23]

While Wylie rejects "automatic" epistemic privilege, she does suggest that some experiences, by virtue of social location, can result in knowledge not otherwise accessible to those who do not share those same experiences from that social location. She explains that when the standpoints of the economically dispossessed, politically oppressed, or socially marginalized are taken into account, often the "epistemic tables are turned." Those who are regarded as epistemically incompetent, because they are considered uneducated, uninformed, unreliable, irrational, overly emotional, and so on, often have the capacity, in virtue of their social location, "to know things that those occupying privileged positions typically do not know, or are invested in not knowing"[24]—or are invested in systematically ignoring or denying. This is because the marginalized have a "bottom-up" perspective, or they possess what Medina, following Du Bois, calls a "double consciousness."

As Medina explains, this double consciousness "involves the capacity to entertain two perspectives, two ways of thinking, and two ways of looking at the world. . . . [It] brings with it the *opportunity* to develop the ability to shift back and forth between two ways of seeing, and hence the ability to make comparisons and contrasts between . . . perspectives."[25] The experience of marginalization affords the opportunity to go beyond the dominant group's perspective, to recognize its limitations and its flaws, and to develop an alternative standpoint or perhaps even, as Medina proposes, a "kaleidoscopic" consciousness, which can allow multiple perspectives.

Susan Heckman argues that the central problem facing standpoint theory today just is this inclusion of multiple perspectives. She asks (rhetorically), "Given multiple standpoints, the social construction of 'reality,' and the necessity of an engaged political position, how can we talk about 'better accounts of the world,' 'less false stories'? And, indeed, how can we talk about accounts of the world at all if the multiplicity of standpoints is, quite literally, endless?"[26] In response to Heckman's objection, I will argue that, in our debate anyway, the survivors *are* the real moral experts (and not the so-called "expert" researchers and medical ethicists), and so they *do* offer a better account of the world and a "less false" story among the differing perspectives.

Adopting standpoint theory requires making a (moral/political) commitment to take the survivors seriously, which heretofore has never been done. It requires trying to understand their point of view no matter how contestable (or even detestable) that point of view might be. Survivors' perspectives, survivors' knowledges, are not articulated or voiced in the "proper" way.

They are knowledges without the accepted credentials, as Medina would say. Following Foucault, he calls them "subjugated knowledges," "knowledges from below," and "unqualified or even disqualified" knowledges, which lack sanction or pedigree.

It is time that we finally legitimize the survivors' voices, even help them speak, especially since their history has taught them that it is dangerous to become visible, dangerous to be heard, and since they undoubtedly feel ambivalent about speaking, knowing that their voices can be so easily drowned out by the scientific and medical ethics communities and cast into "epistemic limbo."[27] Sketching out the claims that standpoint theory might make with respect to our debate, we arrive at the following:

1. Despite that survivors are judged to be epistemically incompetent, they have epistemic insight, grounded in their experiences, which the so-called experts (those who are deemed epistemically competent) lack. As a result, survivors can provide new critical questions and relevant information unique to their subjective experiences, which can change the direction of our debate. For example, our debate, when controlled by the dominant group (of "experts"), has centered on whether it is ethical to use the data, but when we take the survivors' voices seriously, the debate shifts. The question now becomes who should make such decisions. Whether we should use the data becomes secondary. Of course, the only way that the survivors' message will get through is if the "experts" exercise epistemic humility. As Medina notes, epistemic humility—being attentive to one's cognitive limitations and deficits (so long as it does not become crippling)—is a virtue. However, doing so might be morally and intellectually "disturbing," since it challenges the accepted paradigm and the reasonableness of their assumptions and practices. Indeed, it challenges their very interpretation of reality.
2. However well-intentioned the "experts" are in our debate, some of the most important (and morally relevant) considerations are not visible to them. This is because they operate at the level of theory, brute facts, and arguments (which they take to be "reasonable," but which really only privilege and protect their values and interests). By operating at this level, they cannot see, or refuse to accept (because it does not "fit"), the survivors' emotionally laden perspective. By posing the survivors' perspective against theories, facts, and arguments, I do not suggest that survivors cannot have theories, facts, or arguments (indeed they do), but that the so-called experts do not recognize them as such, because they differ from the accepted paradigm.
3. Since the so-called experts are the ones in power, they "structure" the debate in which the survivors participate. That is, when the survivors

participate, they must do so on the experts' terms and in their "living room" so to speak. The "experts" define the conditions and language of the debate. They determine what counts as "rational" and "irrational." According to their paradigm, rational claims are made "coolly," without passion—they are coherent, objective, and accessible to all. Those claims that are emotional, perspectival, and accessible only to a few (namely, the survivors' claims) are deemed suspect. The "experts" presume that theory is accessible and applicable to all—that at the level of theory all can participate in our debate equally. Yet the survivors know that at this level they are not equal participants since their "theories" (because emotionally charged) are readily cast into epistemic limbo. Those who are regarded as equals in our debate are the educated, articulate, "rational" ones—the researchers, medical ethicists, and other recognized "experts," who have the accepted credentials.

4. The survivors see "below the surface" of the debate. That is, when they participate, they are forced to operate on the so-called experts' terms, yet they also know what is really going on (what the data really means; how it affects them and the community). As a result, they are able to shift back and forth between these two perspectives. In this way, they reveal the perversions of the debate, its limitations, and its flaws. The survivors offer "practical" knowledge, "unarticulated" knowledge, and "experiential" knowledge, not recognized or legitimized by the so-called experts. But this leaves the "experts" epistemically and morally impoverished. We should take seriously the claims of the *real* moral experts in our case; in particular, *we should defer to their expertise and trust their testimony.*

As John Hardwig notes, most epistemologists seem to believe that knowledge rests on evidence, not trust.[28] However, this supposition is badly mistaken. In most disciplines, including the sciences, we come to know by trusting others, and in particular, by trusting others' expertise. That is, even in the scientific disciplines, we trust others' testimony as an important source of knowledge. Hardwig defends knowledge by testimony especially in situations where a given person, say Anna, either does not or cannot have another person's, say Bernard's, reasons to believe/know some proposition.[29] On Hardwig's model, Anna is justified in believing Bernard's testimony on his say-so when she believes (and has good reasons to believe) that Bernard (unlike Anna) is in a position to know what would be good reasons to believe that proposition, and Anna believes that Bernard actually has those reasons, and he speaks truthfully.

Importantly, Anna's reliance on Bernard's testimony means that she relies on his moral character (specifically, that he is trustworthy), but also on his epistemic character (that he is competent and conscientious). That is, Anna must trust Bernard, and he must be trustworthy. Hardwig notes that this results in an epistemologically odd conclusion: "The rationality of many of our beliefs depends not only on our own character, but on the character of others as well."[30] In our debate, the survivors' trustworthiness is suspect because they are taken to be emotional cripples. I have argued that the survivors are not *really* untrustworthy, but just that the "experts" think so, given their paradigm of "cool rationality."

In our debate, the survivors have good reasons to believe, given their proximity to the data, that (1) the data is evil; (2) using the data, especially without their consent, harms them; and (3) it harms our community. Further, the researchers and medical ethicists would be rational to accept the survivors' claims to knowledge in this case, because survivors have good moral and epistemic character. Indeed, in accepting the survivors' claims (*should* they accept the survivors' claims, and we saw why it is difficult for them to do so), the researchers and medical ethicists come to have moral knowledge that would be otherwise inaccessible to them.

Hardwig notes that another strategy for ascertaining a person's moral and epistemic reliability is by way of corroboration: If Carlos, Devin, and Erika can corroborate Bernard's testimony, then Anna will have another good reason to believe it.[31] This criterion is also met in our debate, since many survivors have made similar claims about the data and the harm done by our using it.

Since we trust the testimony of scientific authorities, and authorities in other disciplines, why do we seem to set higher standards with respect to moral testimony? Julia Driver argues that this is because there is more "cost" in accepting moral testimony then, say, aesthetic testimony. As she puts it, "I'm free to thumb my nose at Martha Stewart, but not so in the case of the moral expert."[32]

Some people are suspicious about the entire enterprise of moral knowledge, moral testimony, and moral expertise. Robert Hopkins argues against these so-called pessimists who claim that we should never rely on moral testimony. That is, while it is "widely accepted that a good deal of what we believe, we believe on the say-so of others," many are skeptical about whether testimony can be a legitimate source of *moral* belief.[33]

Some pessimists reject that we should rely on the moral testimony of others because they do not believe that there is such thing as moral knowledge in the first place. Morality is at best a matter of opinion and at worst a matter of feeling. Testimony cannot transmit moral knowledge, since there is no such thing as moral knowledge. Against this, Hopkins recognizes that "whatever the status of moral claims, there is certainly room, in moral matters, for something like scrutiny and deliberation," and moral testimony can serve an important role here.[34] Further, we all make "moral" decisions, regardless of what we consider the epistemic status of moral matters to be.

Another reason that some pessimists reject that we should rely on the moral testimony of others is that moral matters are "always sufficiently important to require thinking through for oneself."[35] Alison Hills argues in this way. Our goal should be to acquire what she calls "moral understanding," which involves grasping reasons why a moral proposition is true and being able to draw appropriate conclusions about similar cases.[36] Given that this should be our goal, "we have strong reasons neither to trust moral testimony nor to defer to moral experts, though taking moral advice is both acceptable and often very useful."[37] Against this sort of claim, Hopkins argues that, especially in cases where we know ourselves to be unreliable judges on the matter at hand, *we do defer to others* who know more than we do.[38] This is certainly true with respect to non-moral matters, but it is also true with respect to moral ones.

Some pessimists also reject relying on moral testimony because testimony requires expertise. We should only take the word of those who have authority on the matter, or at least who are experts relative to us. But pessimists claim that the idea of *moral* expertise is highly suspect.[39] What makes someone a moral expert? And who would do the credentialing? In answer to these doubts, Hopkins notes that we need not make the strong claim that whenever we can learn some proposition through testimony, the informant must be an expert *absoluter*. The informant need only be an expert *relative* to the recipient with respect to the matter at hand.

Driver calls this "local expertise." She provides an example: "Mary may have a greater sensitivity to issues of sexism than Dan, and thus be an expert relative to Dan on that issue. Dan may possess a greater sensitivity to potential violations of free speech norms, and thus be an expert relative to Mary on those issues."[40] In both cases, Mary and Dan are in possession of moral knowledge. They are moral experts in their respective areas. In our debate, the survivors possess a greater sensitivity to harm caused when we use the data. Because of their intimate connection to it and because they are paying proper attention, they are the *real* experts in our debate.

Driver explains that not just any experience will do. Rather, it must be experience of *the right sort*. She provides three criteria for the sort of experience that should be privileged with respect to moral judgments. First, we ought to consider the *broadness* of a person's experience. As she explains, "In the moral realm, one might give greater weight to the view of someone who has experienced both freedom and repression regarding which is the preferred mode of existence, and which is to be morally supported or promoted."[41] Similarly, Karen Jones argues that "one way to find out about the value of respect is to ask those who have always been respected; a better way is to ask those who have struggled to win respect and tried to live without it."[42] Second, we should also consider the *depth* of experience. For example, we privilege views on the value of freedom from someone who has worked with refugees for many years, compared with someone who has only done this for a few months or not at all. Third, we should privilege those experiences that are *relevant*. So someone who has actually experienced a tragedy, for example, would have more expertise on that tragedy than someone who has not. As Driver notes, this is because imagination, empathy, and sympathy can only take us so far in moral understanding.

So experiences that are broad, deep, and relevant would be privileged over those that are not. In our debate, the survivors' experiences are broad, deep, and relevant, especially when we compare them to the so-called experts' experiences. Survivors know the experience of dignity and indignity, of having control (autonomy) and then losing it. And so their experiences are broader. They have been subjected to torturous medical experimentation. The researchers and medical ethicists have not. And so their experiences are deeper. And they have experienced tragedy, and in particular, tragedy of the sort relevant to our debate.

Driver explains that when a person who has such broad, deep, and relevant—that is, *direct*—experience makes a claim to moral knowledge we would have good reason to discount the views of people who disagree and lack that type of experience. This gives us at least a *prima facie* reason to discount the researchers' and medical ethicists' claims in our debate and defer to the survivors' claims. Driver notes that experience can sometimes distort one's perceptions, which results in a failure to know (something akin to Goldie's *skewing of the epistemic landscape*). However, this is not true of the survivors in our debate.

Moral experts also have what Jones calls "sharper moral vision." As she explains, "There is a moral analogue of blindness, which is not to be assimilated to being too foolish to follow a moral argument. Those who lack the relevant perceptual skills in a given moral domain must rely on those who have sharper moral vision."[43] Those who have sharper moral vision are especially sensitive to morally important features.[44] In the previous chapter, I argued that paying proper attention (commonly vis-à-vis our emotions) often reveals saliences that might otherwise be missed. The survivors have paid proper attention. As a result, they are sensitive to the morally important features in our debate. Thus the researchers and medical ethicists should rely on the survivors' sharper moral vision. And in any case, they owe them moral deference.

Thomas also argues that there are some things that we can properly understand and appreciate only in the context of real experience.[45] Such experiences put us in the position to know what is otherwise inaccessible. Certain of these experiences ground "local" moral expertise. This is certainly true in our debate. We owe what he calls "moral deference" to those who have such experiences, especially to those who have been (historically) subjected to epistemic injustice. Thomas explains that his concept of moral deference owes its philosophical inspiration to Thomas Nagel's essay "What is it Like to Be a Bat?"[46]

Thomas asks us to imagine that bats are intelligent creatures possessing a natural language—what he calls "batese." As he explains, if we could translate batese, then surely we would take their word for what it is like to be a bat. We would not challenge them, asking them, for example, "Are you *sure* this is what you want to say—that this is *really* what it's like to be a bat?" And if the bats—including the most intelligent and articulate ones—were to say that being a bat "is extraordinarily like experiencing death through colors," we would probably not be able to grasp exactly what is being claimed, but even so, "we would be in no position to dismiss their claims as so much nonsense, just because we cannot fully grasp it."[47] Instead, bats would be owed our deference.

In a way, survivors in our debate also possess their own (emotionally charged) language, which is informed by their experiences. We cannot completely understand it. Their claims might not make any sense to us. They might sound as unintelligible as "death through colors." Even though we cannot grasp what they say, we should not dismiss their claims as so much nonsense just because we do not understand them. But this is precisely what some researchers and medical ethicists have done, and this has resulted in profound harms of the sort that I have articulated throughout this work.

We owe the survivors moral deference. It is time that we take them seriously: as epistemically credible and as offering knowledge of indispensable value in our debate. Not only would we help them heal by restoring their dignity, they are the ones with the sharper moral vision. They are the ones whose emotions have alerted them to (or reminded them of) what truly matters in our debate. They are the ones who see the evil, who see the indignity, who see the harm. The survivors are asking us to let them control the debate. Doing so will help them heal their dignity, restore their *kavod*, and work toward community healing.

I have tried to present the strongest case for the survivors. As moral experts, the survivors possess moral understanding in the sense that Hills describes. In particular, they are able to draw conclusions about similar cases. That is, while we have been focusing on *our* debate, there are many historical cases of data gained by unethical experimentation. Tuskegee and Willowbrook immediately come to mind, but we can multiply examples. If what the survivors have been saying is true, as I have been arguing, then their insights also apply to all similar cases; indeed, to all future cases. Importantly, the survivors see that utility is not the only or the most important consideration in our debate, and they see this through their experiences. Of course experts are not infallible. But we ought to take the survivors seriously for the experts that they are—something that has heretofore never been considered. In this way they (or their surrogates) will be active participants in our debate.

At this point we would have to reopen our debate, perhaps on the survivors' or their families' prompting, for it has largely died out. As I noted in the Introduction, the decision to do nothing (with few exceptions) has kept everything status quo. Another problem is that we cannot unlearn what we know. We also cannot decouple the data from what is already in print. But we can make decisions about *future* uses of it and about new data which we might come across from other unethical sources. Or rather: *Survivors should make such decisions.*

Marcia Angell asks us to consider a hypothetical researcher who wants to test a possible vaccine against HIV infection. Scientifically, the best way to go would be to choose healthy participants, give the vaccine to half of them, and then inject all of them with HIV and compare the infection rates of the two groups. While such research would be simple, fast, and conclusive (we would have a clear answer to the question of whether the vaccine was effective and it would have tremendous public health benefits and save many lives), it would be unethical. We would be treating the experimental subjects like guinea pigs. So instead, our hypothetical researcher must decide to conduct her research ethically, in a much less efficient and conclusive (and much slower) way than simply injecting the virus. Doing the right thing could result in loss of lives—many lives—of people around the globe who contracted HIV but have to wait for a vaccine until our researcher's ethical trial is complete.[48]

Our case is similar. Using the Dachau hypothermia data, for example, would be simple, fast, and conclusive. But it is unethical. If we use the data, we continue to treat survivors like guinea pigs. But we do not treat future hypothermia victims like guinea pigs if we decide not to use the data, even if some (or many) die. This could mean loss of lives for the sake of doing the right thing, just as we expect to lose lives of HIV-infected people for the sake of conducting ethical research.

What I propose is something like a paradigm shift in what we take to be knowledge claims and whom we take to be epistemically credible. The question in the end becomes whether we should trust the claims of the *real* moral experts in our debate. I suggest that we should.

NOTES

1. See Lorraine Code, *Rhetorical Spaces: Essays on Gendered Location* (New York: Routledge, 1995), 27.

2. Myra Giberovitch, *Recovering from Genocidal Trauma: An Information and Practice Guide for Working with Holocaust Survivors* (Toronto: University of Toronto Press, 2014), 52.

3. Miranda Fricker, *Epistemic Injustice: Power and the Ethics of Knowing* (Oxford: Oxford University Press, 2007), 39.

4. Lawrence M. Thomas, "Moral Deference," in *Theorizing Multiculturalism*, ed. Cynthia Willet (New York: Blackwell Press, 1998), 365–66.

5. Miranda Fricker, *Epistemic Injustice: Power and the Ethics of Knowing* (Oxford: Oxford University Press, 2007), 14.

6. *Ibid.*

7. José Medina, *The Epistemology of Resistance: Gender and Racial Oppression, Epistemic Injustice, and Resistant Imaginations* (Oxford: Oxford University Press, 2013), 91.

8. *Ibid.*, 93.

9. *Ibid.*, 111, my emphasis.

10. Dori Laub, "Bearing Witness, or the Vicissitudes of Listening," in *Testimony: Crises of Witnessing in Literature, Psychoanalysis, and History*, eds. Shoshana Felman and Dori Laub (New York: Routledge, 1992), 72–73.

11. Miranda Fricker, *Epistemic Injustice: Power and the Ethics of Knowing* (Oxford: Oxford University Press, 2007), 43.

12. *Ibid.*, 44.

13. *Ibid.*

14. José Medina, *The Epistemology of Resistance: Gender and Racial Oppression, Epistemic Injustice, and Resistant Imaginations* (Oxford: Oxford University Press, 2013), 29.

15. Sandra Harding, "Standpoint Theories: Productively Controversial," *Hypatia* 24, no. 4 (2009): 193.

16. Uma Narayan, "The Project of Feminist Epistemology: Perspectives from a Nonwestern Feminist," in *The Feminist Standpoint Theory Reader*, ed. Sandra Harding (New York: Routledge, 2004), 221.

17. Sandra Harding, "Rethinking Standpoint Epistemology: What Is 'Strong Objectivity'?" in *The Feminist Standpoint Theory Reader*, ed. Sandra Harding (New York: Routledge, 2004), 136–37.

18. Alison Jaggar, "Feminist Politics and Epistemology: The Standpoint of Women," in *The Feminist Standpoint Theory Reader*, ed. Sandra Harding (New York: Routledge, 2004), 56.

19. Alison Wylie, "Why Standpoint Matters," in *The Feminist Standpoint Theory Reader*, ed. Sandra Harding (New York: Routledge, 2004), 343.

20. Sandra Harding, "Rethinking Standpoint Epistemology: What Is 'Strong Objectivity'?" in *The Feminist Standpoint Theory Reader*, ed. Sandra Harding (New York: Routledge, 2004), 128.

21. Uma Narayan, "The Project of Feminist Epistemology: Perspectives from a Nonwestern Feminist," in *The Feminist Standpoint Theory Reader*, ed. Sandra Harding (New York: Routledge, 2004), 214.

22. Sandra Harding, "Standpoint Theories: Productively Controversial," *Hypatia* 24, no. 4 (2009): 194.

23. Alison Wylie, "Why Standpoint Matters," in *The Feminist Standpoint Theory Reader*, ed. Sandra Harding (New York: Routledge, 2004), 339.

24. *Ibid.*, 344.

25. José Medina, *The Epistemology of Resistance: Gender and Racial Oppression, Epistemic Injustice, and Resistant Imaginations* (Oxford University Press, 2013), 29; Sandra Harding, "Standpoint Theories: Productively Controversial," *Hypatia* 24, no. 4 (2009): 192.

26. Susan Heckman, "Truth and Method: Feminist Standpoint Theory Revisited," in *The Feminist Standpoint Theory Reader*, ed. Sandra Harding (New York: Routledge, 2004), 235.

27. See Rachel Josefowitz Siegel, "'I Don't Know Enough': Jewish Women's Learned Ignorance," in *Celebrating the Lives of Jewish Women: Patterns in a Feminist Sampler*, eds. Rachel Josefowitz Siegel and Ellen Cole (New York: Routledge, 1997); and Lorraine Code, *Rhetorical Spaces: Essays on Gendered Location* (New York: Routledge, 1995).

28. John Hardwig, "The Role of Trust in Knowledge," *The Journal of Philosophy* 88, no. 12 (1991): 693.

29. *Ibid.*, 699.

30. *Ibid.*, 700.

31. *Ibid.*, 701.

32. Julia Driver, "Autonomy and the Asymmetry Problem for Moral Expertise," *Philosophical Studies* 128 (2006): 640.

33. Robert Hopkins, "What is Wrong with Moral Testimony," *Philosophy and Phenomenological Research* 74, no. 3 (2007): 611.

34. *Ibid.*, 615–16.

35. *Ibid.*, 621.

36. Alison Hills, "Moral Testimony and Moral Epistemology," *Ethics* 120 (2009): 101–102.

37. *Ibid.*, 98.

38. Robert Hopkins, "What is Wrong with Moral Testimony," *Philosophy and Phenomenological Research* 74, no. 3 (2007): 621–22.

39. *Ibid.*, 623.

40. Julia Driver, "Autonomy and the Asymmetry Problem for Moral Expertise," *Philosophical Studies* 128 (2006): 625.

41. *Ibid.*, 628.

42. Karen Jones, "Second-Hand Moral Knowledge," *The Journal of Philosophy* 96, no. 2 (1999): 65.

43. *Ibid.*, 63.

44. Alison Hills, "Moral Testimony and Moral Epistemology," *Ethics* 120 (2009): 96.

45. Lawrence M. Thomas, "Moral Deference," in *Theorizing Multiculturalism*, ed. Cynthia Willet (New York: Blackwell Press, 1998), 371.

46. Thomas Nagel, "What is it Like to Be a Bat?" *The Philosophical Review* 83, no. 4 (October 1974): 435–50.

47. Thomas, 361.

48. Marcia Angell, "Medical Research: The Dangers to Human Subjects," *The New York Review of Books*, 2015.

Bibliography

Améry, Jean. "Torture." In *Holocaust Religious and Philosophical Implications*, edited by John Roth and Michael Berenbaum. St. Paul, MN: Paragon House, 1989.
———. Quoted in *Approaches to Auschwitz: The Holocaust and its Legacy*, edited by Richard Rubenstein and John K. Roth. Louisville, KY: Westminster John Knox Press, 2003.
———. *At the Mind's Limit: Contemplations by a Survivor on Auschwitz and Its Realities*. Bloomington: Indiana University Press, 2009.
Angell, Marcia. "The Nazi Hypothermia Experiments and Unethical Research Today." *New England Journal of Medicine* 322 (1990): 1462–64.
———. "Editorial Responsibility: Protecting Human Rights by Restricting Publication of Unethical Research." In *The Nazi Doctors and the Nuremberg Code: Human Rights in Human Experimentation*, edited by George Annas and Michael Grodin, 276–85. Oxford: Oxford University Press, 1995.
———. "Medical Research: The Dangers to Human Subjects." *The New York Review of Books*, 2015.
Anonymous. "Learning from a Failure of Western Culture." *Star Tribune*, May 25, 1988.
———. "Data Use an Unforgivable Insult." *Cleveland Jewish News*, May 26, 1989.
Arendt, Hannah. *Origins of Totalitarianism*. New York: Harcourt Brace Jovanovich, 1952.
Armour, Marilyn. "Meaning Making in Survivorship: Applications to Holocaust Survivors." *Journal of Human Behavior in the Social Environment* 20, no. 4 (2010): 440–68.
Banyard, Victoria L. "Trauma and Memory." *PTSD Research Quarterly* 11, no. 4 (2000), at ptsd.va.gov.
Bauer, Yehuda. *A History of the Holocaust*. London: Franklin Watts, 1982.
Bauman, Batya. "Women-Identified Women in Male-Identified Judaism." In *On Being a Jewish Feminist*, edited by Susannah Heschel, 88–95. New York: Schocken Books, 1982.

Bedard, Michele, et al. "Is Trauma Memory Special? Trauma Narrative Fragmentation in PTSD: Effects of Treatment and Response." *Clinical Psychological Science* 5, no. 2 (March 2017): 212–25.

Berger, Robert. "Nazi Science—the Dachau Hypothermia Experiments." *The New England Journal of Medicine* 332, no. 20 (1990): 1435–40.

Bernstein, J. M. *Torture and Dignity: An Essay on Moral Injury*. Chicago: University of Chicago Press, 2015.

Bleich, J. David. "Using Data Obtained Through Immoral Experimentation." In *Medicine and Jewish Law* Volume II, edited by Fred Rosner. Lanham, MD: Jason Aronson, 1993.

Boetzkes, Elizabeth. "Equality, Autonomy, and Feminist Bioethics." In *Embodying Bioethics: Recent Feminist Advances*, edited by Anne Donchin and Laura Purdy, 121–40. Lanham, MD: Roman & Littlefield, 1999.

Bogod, David. "The Nazi Hypothermia Experiments: Forbidden Data." *Anaesthesia* 59, no. 12 (2004): 1155–56.

Bontekoe, Ron. *The Nature of Dignity*. Lanham, MD: Lexington Books, 2008.

Borowski, Tadeusz. *This Way for the Gas, Ladies and Gentleman*. Translated by Barbara Vedder and Michael Kandel. New York: Penguin Classics, 1992.

Bowers, Mallory E., and Rachel Yehuda. "Intergenerational Transmission of Stress in Humans." *Neuropsychopharmacology REVIEWS* 41 (2016): 232–44.

Brady, Michael. "Emotions, Perceptions, and Reasons." In *Morality and the Emotions*, edited by Carla Bagnoli, 135–49. Oxford: Oxford University Press, 2011.

———. *Emotional Insight: The Epistemic Role of Emotional Experience*. Oxford: Oxford University Press, 2013.

Brecht, Bertolt. "I, the Survivor." In *Bertolt Brecht: A Literary Life*, edited by Stephen Parker, 438. London: Methuen Drama, 2015.

Brenner, Rachel. "Teaching the Holocaust in the Academia: Educational Mission(s) and Pedagogical Approaches." *Journal of Holocaust Education* 8, no. 2 (1999): 1–26.

Brison, Susan J. "Outliving Oneself: Trauma, Memory, and Personal Identity." In *Feminists Rethink the Self*, edited by Diana T. Myers. Boulder, CO: Westview Press, 1996.

Broner, E. M. *A Weave of Women*. Bloomington: Indiana University Press, 1985.

Caplan, Arthur. Quoted in Mike Steele, "Conference Will Study Holocaust and Bioethics." *Star Tribune*, May 17, 1989.

———. Quoted in Jim Fuller, "Holocaust Casts Lasting Shadows on Science." *Star Tribune*, May 18, 1989.

———. "The Meaning of the Holocaust for Bioethics." *Hastings Center Report* 19, no. 4 (August 1989): 2–3.

Card, Claudia. *The Unnatural Lottery: Character and Moral Luck*. Philadelphia: Temple University Press, 1996.

———. *The Atrocity Paradigm: A Theory of Evil*. Oxford: Oxford University Press, 2002.

Caruth, Cathy. *Unclaimed Experience: Trauma, Narrative, and History*. Baltimore: Johns Hopkins University Press, 1996.

Cisneros, Sandra. *The House on Mango Street*. New York: Vintage Books, 1984.
Code, Lorraine. *Rhetorical Spaces: Essays on Gendered Location*. New York: Routledge, 1995.
Coetzee, J. M. *Elizabeth Costello*. New York: Penguin Books, 2003.
Cook, Lindsey. "Why Black Americans Die Younger." *US News and World Report*, January 5, 2015.
Danto, Arthur. "the naked truth." In *Aesthetics and Ethics: Essays at the Intersection (Cambridge Studies in Philosophy and the Arts)*, revised edition, edited by Jerrold Levinson, 257–82. Cambridge: Cambridge University Press, 2001.
De Beauvoir, Simone. *The Second Sex*. Translated by H. M. Parshley. New York: Random House, 1952.
Dekel, Sharon Dekel, and George Bonanno. "Changes in Trauma Memory: Patterns of Posttraumatic Stress." *Psychological Trauma: Theory, Research, Practice and Policy* 5, no. 1 (2013): 26–34.
Delbo, Charlotte. *Auschwitz and After*. Translated Rosette C. Lamont. New Haven, CT: Yale University Press, 1995.
Des Pres, Terrence. "Excremental Assault." In *Holocaust Religious and Philosophical Implications*, edited by John Roth and Michael Berenbaum. St. Paul, MN: Paragon House, 1989.
Driver, Julia. "Autonomy and the Asymmetry Problem for Moral Expertise. " *Philosophical Studies* 128, no. 3 (2006): 619–44.
Falkner, Brian, and Arthur Hafner. "Commentary"; "Case Studies: Nazi Data: Dissociation from Evil," *Hastings Center Report* 14, no. 4 (July–August 1989).
Feldman, Irving. "To the Six Million." In *Truth and Lamentation*, edited by Milton Teichman and Sharon Leder, 461–66. Champaign: University of Illinois Press, 1994.
Felman, Shoshana, and Dori Laub. *Testimony: Crisis of Witnessing in Literature, Psychoanalysis, and History*. New York: Routledge, 1992.
Figley, Charles R., ed. *Compassion Fatigue: Coping with Secondary Traumatic Stress Disorder in Those Who Treat the Traumatized*. New York: Routledge, 2015.
Fine, Ellen S. "Dialogue with Elie Wiesel." *Centerpoint: A Journal of Interdisciplinary Studies* 4, no. 1 (Fall 1980).
Frankl, Viktor. *Man's Search for Meaning*. New York: Simon and Schuster, 1959.
Freedman, Benjamin. Quoted in "Scientists Say Holocaust Should Have Taught That Science Alone Falls Short." *Star Tribune*, May 19, 1989.
———. "Moral Analysis and the Use of Nazi Experimental Results." In *When Medicine Went Mad: Bioethics and the Holocaust*, edited by Arthur Caplan, 141–54. New York: Humana Press, 1992.
Freedman, Monroe, et al. "Nazi Research Too Evil to Cite." *Hastings Center Report* 15, no. 4 (August 1985): 31–32.
Fricker, Miranda. *Epistemic Injustice: Power and the Ethics of Knowing*. Oxford: Oxford University Press, 2007.
Friday, Jonathan. "Transparency and the Photographic Image." *The British Journal of Aesthetics* 36, no. 1 (1996): 30–42.

Garver, Newton. "What Violence Is." In *Social Ethics: Morality and Social Policy*, edited by Thomas Mappes and James Zembaty. New York: McGraw-Hill, 1977.

Gaylin, Willard. "Commentary" ; "Case Studies: Nazi Data: Dissociation from Evil," *Hastings Center Report* 14, no. 4 (July–August 1989).

Giberovitch, Myra. *Recovering from Genocidal Trauma: An Information and Practice Guide for Working with Holocaust Survivors*. Toronto: University of Toronto Press, 2014.

Goldie, Peter. "Emotion, Reason, and Virtue." In *Emotion, Evolution, and Rationality*, edited by Dylan Evans and Pierre Cruse, 249–68. Oxford: Oxford University Press, 2004.

Goodman, Lenn E. "Toward a Jewish Philosophy of Justice." In *Commandment and Community: New Essays in Jewish Legal and Political Philosophy*, edited by Daniel Frank, 3–54. Albany, NY: SUNY Press, 1995.

Gorovitz, Samuel. "Procurement and Allocation of Human Organs for Transplantation." *Hearings before the Subcommittee on Investigations and Oversight of the Committee on Science and Technology*, Ninety-Eighth Congress, First Session, No. 71, 1983.

Gotfryd, Bernard. "Reunions." In *Images from the Holocaust: A Literature Anthology*, edited by Jean Brown, et al. Lincolnwood, IL: NTC Publishing Group, 1996.

Greene, Velvl. "Can Scientists Use Information Derived from the Concentration Camps? Ancient Answers to New Questions." In *When Medicine Went Mad: Bioethics and the Holocaust*, edited by Arthur Caplan, 155–72. New York: Humana Press, 1992.

Griffin, John. *Black Like Me*. New York: Signet Books, 1996.

Gwyther, Matthew, and Sean McConville. "Nazi Experiments: Can Good Come from Evil?" *London Observer*, November 19, 1989.

Hamblen, Jessica, et al. "Overview of Psychotherapy for PTSD" at ptsd.va.gov.

Harding, Sandra. *Whose Science? Whose Knowledge?* Ithaca, NY: Cornell University Press, 1991.

———. "Rethinking Standpoint Epistemology: What Is 'Strong Objectivity'?" In *The Feminist Standpoint Reader: Intellectual and Political Controversies*, edited by Sandra Harding, 127–40. New York: Routledge, 2004.

———. "Standpoint Theories: Productively Controversial," *Hypatia* 24, no. 4 (2009): 192–200.

Hardwig, John. "The Role of Trust in Knowledge." *The Journal of Philosophy* 88, no. 12 (1991): 693–708.

Hare, R. M. "What is Wrong with Slavery?" In *Applied Ethics*, edited by Peter Singer. Oxford: Oxford University Press, 1986.

Heckman, Susan. "Truth and Method: Feminist Standpoint Theory Revisited." In *The Feminist Standpoint Reader: Intellectual and Political Controversies*, edited by Sandra Harding, 225–42. New York: Routledge, 2004.

Herman, Judith. *Trauma and Recovery: The Aftermath of Violence—From Domestic Abuse to Political Terror*. New York: Basic Books, 1997.

Hill, Thomas. *Dignity and Practical Reason in Kant's Moral Theory*. Ithaca, NY: Cornell University Press, 1992.

Hills, Alison. "Moral Testimony and Moral Epistemology." *Ethics* 120, no. 1 (2009): 94–127.
Hirsch, Marianne. "Marked by Memory: Feminist Reflections on Trauma and Transmission." In *Extremities: Trauma, Testimony, and* Community, edited by Nancy K. Miller and Jason Tougaw, 71–91. Champaign: University of Illinois Press, 2002.
Hobbes, Thomas. *Leviathan*. Edited by Edwin Curley. Indianapolis: Hackett Publishing, 1994.
Holmes, Helen Bequaert. "Closing the Gaps: An Imperative for Feminist Bioethics." In *Embodying Bioethics: Recent Feminist Advances*, edited by Anne Donchin and Laura Purdy. Lanham, MD: Rowman & Littlefield, 1999.
hooks, bell. *Feminist Theory: From Margin to Center*. Boston: South End Press, 1984.
Hopkins, Robert. "What is Wrong with Moral Testimony." *Philosophy and Phenomenological Research* 74, no. 3 (2007): 611–34.
Hudnall Stamm, Beth, ed. *Secondary Traumatic Stress: Self-Care Issues for Clinicians, Researchers, and Educators*. Brooklandville, MD: Sidran Institute Press, 1999.
Ingraham, Christopher. "Our Infant Mortality Rate is a National Embarrassment." *Washington Post*, September 29, 2014.
Iuculano, John, and Keith Burkum. "The Humanism of Sartre: Toward a Psychology of Dignity." *Journal of Theoretical and Philosophical Psychology* 16, no. 1 (1996): 19–29.
Jaggar, Alison. "Feminist Politics and Epistemology: The Standpoint of Women." In *The Feminist Standpoint Reader: Intellectual and Political Controversies*, edited by Sandra Harding, 55–66. New York: Routledge, 2004.
Janoff-Bulman, Ronnie. *Shattered Assumptions: Towards a New Psychology of Trauma*. New York: Free Press, 1992.
Jones, John D. *Poverty and the Human Condition: A Philosophical Inquiry*. New York: Edwin Mellen Press, 1990.
Jones, Karen. "Second-Hand Moral Knowledge." *The Journal of Philosophy* 96, no. 2 (1999): 55–78.
Jordan, Nicolle. "A Creole Contagion: Narratives of Slavery and Tainted Wealth in *Millennium Hall*." *Tulsa Studies in Women's Literature* 30, no. 1 (2011): 57–70.
Kant, Immanuel. *Observations on the Feeling of the Beautiful and Sublime*. Translated by John Goldthwait. Berkeley: University of California Press, 1960.
———. *Groundwork of the Metaphysics of Morals*. Translated by H. J. Paton. New York: Harper and Row, 1964.
———. *The Doctrine of Virtue*. Translated by Mary J. Gregor. New York: Harper and Row, 1964.
Katz, Jay. "Untitled." *Long Island Jewish World Newsletter*, July 4, 1989.
Katz, Jay, and Robert Pozos. "The Dachau Hypothermia Study: An Ethical and Scientific Commentary." In *When Medicine Went Mad: Bioethics and the Holocaust*, edited by Arthur Caplan, 135–40. New York: Humana Press, 1992.
Kellermann, Natan P. F. "Transmission of Holocaust Trauma—An Integrative View." *Psychiatry* 64, no. 3 (2001): 256–67.

———. *Holocaust Trauma: Psychological Effects and Treatment*. New York: iUniverse Inc., 2009.

Kirman, Joseph. "Doves on Wires." In *Truth and Lamentation: Stories and Poems on the Holocaust*, edited by Milton Teichman and Sharon Leder, 212. Champaign: University of Illinois Press, 1994.

Konopka, Gisela. "Holocaust Survivor Questions Data's Validity." *The Minnesota Daily*, July 27, 1988.

Kor, Eva Mozes. Quoted in Matthew Gwyther and Sean McConville "Nazi Experiments: Can Good Come from Evil?" *London Observer*, November 19, 1989.

———. "Nazi Experiments as Viewed by a Survivor of Mengele's Experiments." In *When Medicine Went Mad: Bioethics and the Holocaust*, edited by Arthur Caplan, 3–8. New York: Humana Press, 1992.

Lancaster, Cynthia, et al. "Posttraumatic Stress Disorder: Overview of Evidence Based Assessment and Treatment." *Journal of Clinical Medicine* 5, no. 11 (November 2016). Available at http://www.mdpi.com/2077-0383/5/11/105/htm

Langer, Lawrence. "Interpreting Survivors' Testimonies." In *Writing and the Holocaust*, edited by Berel Lang. New York: Holmes and Meier Publishers, 1984.

———. "The Dilemma of Choice in the Death Camps." In *Holocaust: Religious and Philosophical Implications*, edited by John Roth and Michael Berenbaum. St Paul, MN: Paragon House, 1989.

———. *Holocaust Testimonies: The Ruins of Memory*. New Haven, CT: Yale University Press, 1991.

———. *Art from the Ashes: A Holocaust Anthology*. New York: Oxford University Press, 1995.

Laub, Dori. "Bearing Witness, or the Vicissitudes of Listening." In *Testimony: Crises of Witnessing in Literature, Psychoanalysis, and History*, edited by Shoshana Felman and Dori Laub, 57–74. New York: Routledge, 1992.

Leiter, Robert. "Untitled." *Long Island Jewish World Newsletter*, July 4, 1989.

Leitner, Isabella. "Saving the Fragments." In *Images from the Holocaust: A Literature Anthology*, edited by Jean Brown, et al. Lincolnwood, IL: NTC Publishing Group, 1996.

Leivick, H. "I Hear a Voice." In *Truth and Lamentation*, edited by Milton Teichman and Sharon Leder, 72. Champaign: University of Illinois Press, 1994.

Levi, Primo. "If Not Now, When? Survival in Auschwitz." In *Images from the Holocaust: A Literature Anthology*, edited by Jean Brown, et al. Lincolnwood, IL: NTC Publishing Group, 1996.

Lorde, Audre. "The Uses of Anger: Women Responding to Racism." In *Sister Outsider*, 124–33. Toronto: Crossing Press, 1984.

Macklin, Ruth. "Dignity is a Useless Concept." *British Medical Journal* 327 (2003): 1419–20.

Martin, Robert. "Using Nazi Scientific Data." *Dialogue* XXV, no. 3 (1986): 403–11.

McCann, Lisa, and Laurie Anne Pearlman. "Vicarious Traumatization: A Framework for Understanding the Psychological Effects of Working with Victims." *Journal of Traumatic Stress* 3, no. 1 (1990): 131–49.

McElwee, Sean. "Six Ways America is Like a Third World Country." *Rolling Stone*, March 5, 2014.
Medina, José. *The Epistemology of Resistance: Gender and Racial Oppression, Epistemic Injustice, and Resistant Imaginations*. Oxford: Oxford University Press, 2013.
Merleau-Ponty, Maurice. *Phenomenology of Perception*. Translated by Donald A. Landes. New York: Routledge, 2012.
Meyer, Michael. "Dignity, Rights, and Self Control." *Ethics* 99, no. 3 (1989): 520–34.
———. "Dignity, Death, and Modern Virtue." *American Philosophical Quarterly* 32, no. 1 (1995).
Mitscherlich, Alexander. *The Death Doctors*. Translated by James Cleugh. London: Elek Books Ltd, 1962.
Mitscherlich, A., and F. Mielke. *Doctor of Infamy: The Story of the Nazi Medical Crimes*. New York: Henry Schuman, 1949.
Moe, Kristine. "Should the Nazi Research Data Be Cited?" *The Hastings Center Report* 14, no. 6 (1984): 5–7.
Munzer, Stephen. "An Uneasy Case Against Property Rights in Body Parts." *Social Philosophy and Policy Foundation* (1994).
Murdoch, Iris. *The Italian Girl*. New York: Vintage, 2000.
Nagel, Thomas. "What is it Like to Be a Bat?" *The Philosophical Review* 83, no. 4 (October 1974): 435–50.
Narayan, Uma. "The Project of Feminist Epistemology: Perspectives from a Nonwestern Feminist." In *The Feminist Standpoint Reader: Intellectual and Political Controversies*, edited by Sandra Harding, 213–24. New York: Routledge, 2004.
Nietzsche, Friedrich. *The Gay Science*, Book III, Aphorism 115. Translated by Josefine Nauckhoff and Adrian Del Caro. Cambridge: Cambridge University Press, 2001.
Nolan, Kathy. Quoted in "When Research is Evil." *Minnesota Alumni Association* (November–December 1988).
Nussbaum, Martha. *Love's Knowledge: Essays on Philosophy and Literature*. Oxford: Oxford University Press, 1990.
Oneill, Onora. "Reasons and Persons." In *Right Conduct: Theories and Applications*, edited by Michael Bayless. New York: Random House, 1983.
Pagis, Dan. "Draft of a Reparations Agreement." In *Holocaust Poetry*, edited by Hilda Schiff, 132. New York: St. Martin's Press, 1995.
Pearlman, Laurie Anne, and Karen W. Saakvitne. *Trauma and the Therapist: Countertransference and Vicarious Traumatization in Psychotherapy with Incest Survivors*. New York: W. W. Norton and Company, 1995.
———. "Treating Therapists with Vicarious Traumatization and Secondary Traumatic Stress Disorders." In *Compassion Fatigue: Coping with Secondary Traumatic Stress Disorder in Those Who Treat the Traumatized*, edited by Charles R. Figley, 150–77. New York: Routledge, 2015.
Perechodnik, Calel. *Am I a Murderer? Testament of a Jewish Ghetto Policeman*. Edited and translated by Frank Fox. Boulder, CO: Westview Press, 1996.
Pillwein, Fritz. "Testimony at the Nuremberg Trials of War Criminals, the Medical Case, Document 912." In *The Death Doctors*, edited by Alexander Mitscherlich, translated by James Cleugh. London: Elek Books Ltd, 1962.

Post, Stephen. "The Echo of Nuremberg: Nazi Data and Ethics." *Journal of Medical Ethics* 17 (1991): 42–44.

Pozos, Robert. Letter to Dr. Judith Bellin. US EPA document. August 2, 1988.

———. Quoted in "When Research is Evil." *Minnesota Alumni Association* (November–December 1988).

Proctor, Robert. Quoted in "Scientists Say Holocaust Should Have Taught that Science Alone Falls Short." *Star Tribune*, May 19, 1989.

Rascher, Sigmond. Letter dated May 15, 1941. "Document 1602 of the Nuremberg Trials of War Criminals: The Medical Case." In *The Death Doctors*, edited by Alexander Mitscherlich, translated by James Cleugh. London: Elek Books Ltd, 1962.

Reznikoff, Charles. *Holocaust*. Boston: Black Sparrow Press, 2007.

Rolston, Holmes. *Environmental Ethics: Duties to and Values in the Natural World*. Philadelphia: Temple University Press, 1988.

Romdenh-Romluc, Komarine. *Routledge Philosophy Guidebook to Merleau-Ponty and Phenomenology of Perception*. New York: Routledge, 2011.

Roth, John. "Reflections on Post-Holocaust Ethics." In *Problems Unique to the Holocaust*, edited by Harry James Cargas, 169–81. Lexington: University of Kentucky Press, 1999.

Roth, Sol. *The Jewish Idea of Culture*. Hoboken, NJ: KTAV Publishing House, 1997.

Rothberg, Michael. "Between the Extreme and the Everyday: Ruth Klüger's Traumatic Realism." In *Extremities: Trauma, Testimony, and Community*, edited by Nancy K. Miller and Jason Tougaw, 55–70. Champaign: University of Illinois Press, 2002.

Rousseau, Jean-Jacques. *The Social Contract and Other Later Political Writings*. Translated by Victor Gourevitch. Cambridge: Cambridge University Press, 1997.

Rousset, David. "The Dead Stars Pursue their Courses." In *Holocaust: Religious and Philosophical Implications*, edited by John Roth and Michael Berenbaum. St. Paul, MN: Paragon House, 1989.

Rubenstein, Richard. "An Exchange." In *Holocaust: Religious and Philosophical Implications*, edited by John Roth and Michael Berenbaum. St. Paul, MN: Paragon House, 1989.

Sachs, Nelly. "Chorus of the Rescued." In *Art from the Ashes: A Holocaust Anthology*, edited by Lawrence L. Langer, 643. New York: Oxford University Press, 1995.

Sarton, May. *As We Are Now*. Quoted in Lorraine Code, *Rhetorical Spaces: Essays on Gendered Location*. New York: Routledge, 1995.

Schafer, Arthur. "On Using the Nazi Data: The Case Against." *Dialogue* XXV, no. 3 (1986): 413–19.

Scharf, Miri. "Long-Term Effects of Trauma: Psychosocial Functioning of the Second and Third Generation of Holocaust Survivors." *Development and Psychopathology* 19 (2007): 603–22.

Seeskin, Kenneth. "Coming to Terms with Failure: A Philosophical Dilemma." In *Writing and the Holocaust*, edited by Berel Lang. New York: Holmes and Meier Publishers, 1988.

Semprun, Jorge. *What a Beautiful Sunday.* Translated by Alan Sheridan. New York: Harcourt Brace Jovanovich, 1982.
Sen, Amartya. *Development as Freedom.* New York: Random House, 2000.
Sherwin, Susan. "Feminism and Bioethics." In *Feminism and Bioethics, Beyond Reproduction,* edited by Susan Wolf, 47–66. Oxford: Oxford University Press, 1996.
Sholiton, Faye. "Scientific Community Wrestles with Using Tainted Data." *Cleveland Jewish News,* November 25, 1988.
Siegel, Barry. "Can Evil Beget Good?" *Los Angeles Times,* October 20, 1988.
Siegel, Rachel Josefowitz. "'I Don't Know Enough': Jewish Women's Learned Ignorance." In *Celebrating the Lives of Jewish Women: Patterns in a Feminist Sampler,* edited by Rachel Josefowitz Siegel and Ellen Cole, 201–10. New York: Routledge, 1997.
Singer, Peter. *Animal Liberation.* New York: Random House, 1975.
Stauffer, Jill. *Ethical Loneliness: The Injustice of Not Being Heard.* New York: Columbia University Press, 2015.
Stiffel, Frank. "The Tale of the Ring: A Kaddish." In *Images from the Holocaust: A Literature Anthology,* edited by Jean Brown, et al. Lincolnwood, IL: NTC Publishing Group, 1996.
Stocker, Michael, and Elizabeth Hegeman. *Valuing Emotions.* Cambridge: Cambridge University Press, 1996.
Stoller, Sylvia. "Reflections on Feminist Merleau-Ponty Skepticism." *Hypatia* 15, no. 1 (2000): 175–82.
Stone, Christopher. "Should Trees Have Standing? Toward Legal Rights for Natural Objects." In *Environmental Ethics: Readings in Theory and Application,* edited by Louis Pojman, 294–305. Belmont, CA: Wadsworth Publishing, 1998.
Sullivan, Shannon. "Domination and Dialogue in Merleau-Ponty's Phenomenology of Perception." *Hypatia* 12, no. 1 (1997): 1–19.
———. *Living Across and through Skins: Transactional Bodies, Pragmatism, and Feminism.* Bloomington: Indiana University Press, 2001.
Taylor, Charles. *Sources of the Self: The Making of Modern Identity.* Cambridge, MA: Harvard University Press, 1989.
———. "The Politics of Recognition." In *Multiculturalism: A Critical Reader,* edited by David Theo Goldberg, 75–106. Hoboken, NJ: Wiley-Blackwell, 1995.
Thomas, Laurence M. "The Grip of Immorality: Child Abuse and Moral Failure." In *Reason, Ethics, and Society: Themes from Kurt Baier, With His Responses,* edited by J. B. Schneewind, 144–67. Chicago: Open Court Publishing, 1996.
———. "Moral Deference." In *Theorizing Multiculturalism: A Guide to the Current Debate,* edited by Cynthia Willet, 359–81. New York: Blackwell Press, 1998.
United States Environmental Protection Agency. "Mathematical Dose-Response Modeling of Health Effects Potentially Resulting from Air Emissions of Phosgene." August 31, 1987.
Vigorito, Susan. "Far from Emotional Cripples, We Survivors of the Holocaust Have a Clearer Understanding." *Cleveland Jewish News,* May 26, 1989.
———. Quoted in *Long Island Jewish World Newsletter,* July 4, 1989.

Vuilleumier, P., J. Armony, and R. Dolon. "Reciprocal Links Between Emotion and Attention." In *Human Brain Function*, 2nd edition, edited by R. S. J. Frackowiak, et al., 419–44. San Diego, CA: Academic Press, 2003.

Walker, Margaret Urban. "Picking Up Pieces." In *Feminists Rethink the Self*, edited by Diana Tietjens Meyer. Boulder, CO: Westview Press, 1997.

Walton, Kendall. "Transparent Pictures: On the Nature of Photographic Realism." *Critical Inquiry* 11, no. 2 (1984): 246–77.

Warburton, Nigel. "Seeing Through 'Seeing Through Photographs.'" *Ratio* 1, no. 1 (1988): 64–74.

Weiss, Gail. "The Anonymous Intentions of Transactional Bodies." *Hypatia* 17, no. 4 (2002): 187–200.

Wiesel, Elie. *Night*. Translated by Stella Rodway. New York: Avon, 1969.

Wiesel, Elie, and Richard Rubenstein. "An Exchange." In *Holocaust: Religious and Philosophical Implications*, edited by John Roth and Michael Berenbaum. St. Paul, MN: Paragon House, 1989.

Wiesenthal, Simon. *The Sunflower: On the Possibilities and Limits of Forgiveness*. New York: Schocken Press, 1998.

Wilkerson, Isabel. "Nazi Data and Ethics of Today." *New York Times*, May 21, 1989.

Wiseman, Hadas, et al. "Anger, Guilt, and Intergenerational Communication of Trauma in the Interpersonal Narratives of Second Generation Holocaust Survivors." *American Journal of Orthopsychiatry* 76, no. 2 (2006): 176–84.

Witztum, Ely, and Ruth Malkinson. "Examining Traumatic Grief and Loss among Holocaust Survivors." *Journal of Loss and Trauma* 14, no. 2 (2009): 129–43.

Wolf, Stephanie. "Art, or Invasion of Privacy: Photographer Arne Svenson's MCA Exhibit Raises Eyebrows." *Colorado Public Radio* at cpr.org (May 27, 2016).

Wylie, Alison. "Why Standpoint Matters." In *The Feminist Standpoint Reader: Intellectual and Political Controversies*, edited by Sandra Harding, 339–52. New York: Routledge, 2004.

Yehuda, Rachel. "Posttraumatic Stress Disorder." *The New England Journal of Medicine* (January 2002): 108–14.

Yehuda, Rachel, and L. M. Bierer. "The Relevance of Epigenetics to PTSD: Implications for the DSM-V." *Journal of Trauma Stress* 22 (2009): 427–34.

Yehuda, Rachel, et al., "Relationship between Posttraumatic Stress Disorder Characteristics of Holocaust Survivors and their Adult Offspring." *The American Journal of Psychiatry* 155, no. 6 (June 1998): 841–43.

Yehuda, Rachel, et al., "Influences of Maternal and Paternal PTSD on Epigenetic Regulation of the Glucocorticoid Receptor Gene in Holocaust Survivor Offspring." *American Journal of Psychiatry* 171 (2014): 872–80.

Index

Alexander, Leo, 12
Améry, Jean, 50–51, 60
Angell, Marcia, 23, 129
animal rights, 33
Arendt, Hannah, 40, 71
Armour, Marilyn, 77
autonomy, 38–39, 41, 57, 59, 60, 63, 67–69

Banyard, Victoria L., 5
Bauer, Yehuda, 71, 74
Bauman, Batya, 79
Bazin, André, 107
Bedard-Gilligan, Michelle, 5
Berger, Robert, 13
Bernstein, J. M., 6, 32, 34, 40, 42, 43, 49, 50–51, 71
Boetzkes, Elizabeth, 57
Bogod, David, 18–19
Bonanno, George, 5
Bontekoe, Ron, 49, 61, 62
Borowski, Tadeusz, 71, 72
Bowers, Mallory E., 98–99
Brady, Michael, 100, 101
Brecht, Bertolt, 76
Brenner, Rachel, 70
Brison, Susan, 70, 78
Broner, E. M., 69–70

Canadians, 72
Caplan, Arthur, 1, 12–14
Card, Claudia, 73, 94
Caruth, Cathy, 90, 93, 101–2
Categorical Imperative (Kant), 34
Celan, Paul, 98
Cisneros, Sandra, 54–55
Code, Lorraine, 18, 51, 60
Coetzee, J. M., 94, 108
concentration camp survivor syndrome, 2
consent, 34–35
conspiracy of silence, 7
cultural objects, 89, 90, 91, 92, 93, 95, 97, 104, 105

Dachau hypothermia experiments, 1, 11, 13, 19, 40
Danto, Arthur, 106
De Beauvoir, Simone, 56, 71
Dekel, Sharon, 5
Delbo, Charlotte, 70, 103–4
Descartes, René, 89, 93
Des Pres, Terrence, 29, 51, 53
dignity, 4, 6, 16, 18, 28, 30–43, 49–64, 77, 81, 84, 117
double consciousness, 120, 122
double vision, 120

Driver, Julia, 125–27
Dubois, W. E. B., 120, 122

Eitinger, Leo, 2
emotion, 2, 3, 4, 14, 15, 16, 17, 81, 43, 69, 82–83, 90, 99–103, 121
emotion-proper property, 100
Environmental Protection Agency (EPA), 12–13
epistemic advantage, 115–16, 120, 121
epistemic arrogance, 48, 116
epistemic humility, 123
epistemic injustice, 7, 8, 116–19
epistemic privilege, 116, 122
excremental assault, 53
exposure-based therapies, 82–83
evil, 7, 17, 19, 20–21, 80, 84, 89, 90, 91 93–95, 104, 110

Falkner, Brian, 20
false memory syndrome, 5
feminist standpoint epistemology, 120–24
Frankl, Viktor, xiv, 53
Freedman, Benjamin, 15, 19
Fricker, Miranda, 116–20
Friday, Jonathan, 107

Gauguin, Paul, 55
Garver, Newton, 51–52, 54
Gaylin, Willard, 20
Giberovitch, Myra, 2, 51, 77, 117
Goldie, Peter, 90, 99, 100, 101, 103
Gorovitz, Samuel, 59
Greene, Velvl, 19–20, 23
Griffin, John, 55
guilt, 69, 76, 79, 81, 83, 84

Hafner, Arthur, 20
Hamblin, Jessica, 83
Harding, Sandra, 27, 121
Hardwig, John, 124–25
Hare, R. M., 58
Hayward, John, 20
Heckman, Susan, 122

Henley, William Ernest, 53
Herman, Judith, 3, 6, 67–71, 74, 75, 78, 79
hermeneutical injustice, 119
Hill, Thomas, 36
Hills, Alison, 126
Hinduism, 63
Hirsch, Marianne, 97, 98
Hobbes, Thomas, 35–36, 54, 63
Holmes, Helen Bequaert, 37
hooks, bell, 58
Hopkins, Robert, 125, 126
hypothetical construction, 109

identity prejudice, 118
implicit coercion, 34, 59
integrity, 61, 62
intergenerational trauma, 77, 98–99, 117
intrinsic value, 32–34
inversion, thesis, 121–22

Janoff-Bulman, Ronnie, 6, 37–8, 53, 73–4, 76
Jones, David, 73
Jones, John, 38, 52–3
Jones, Karen, 126, 127
Jordan, Nicolle, 95
just world hypothesis, 73

Kant, Immanuel, 30–43, 63
Karpf, Anne, 98
Katz, Jay, 13
kavod, 6, 18, 47–49, 77, 84, 117
Kellermann, Natan, 2
kingdom of ends (Kant), 36–38, 40, 63
Konopka, Gisela, 21
Kor, Eva Moses, 22, 80

Lancaster, Cynthia, 68, 69, 82, 103
Langer, Lawrence, 16, 17, 30, 47, 52, 67, 70, 71, 72, 76
Laub, Dori, 4, 5, 97, 119
Le Guin, Ursula, 36
Leitner, Isabella, 74
Levi, Primo, 28–29

Index

Lincoln, Abraham, 61
local expertise, 126, 127
Lorde, Audrey, 57, 60

Malkinson, Ruth, 77
Martin, Robert, 21
McCann, Lisa, 102
meaning making, 77, 79, 81, 84
Medina, José, 118–19, 122, 123
mental health profession, 2–3
Merleau-Ponty, Maurice, 89, 90–92,
    95–96, 99, 104–5, 108, 109
Meyer, Michael, 56–57
Minghella, Anthony, 117
moral deference, 127–28
moral expertise, 3, 4, 116, 126, 127
moral knowledge, 125–27
moral taint, 94–95, 110
moral testimony, 125–26
moral understanding, 126, 127
Morrison, Toni, 97
Munzer, Stephen, 42
Murdoch, Iris, 98
Muselmann, 50–51, 71

Nagel, Thomas, 128
Narayan, Uma, 120, 121
Nazi medical experiments, 11
Nolan, Kathy, 22
Nussbaum, Martha, 16, 100

Pagis, Dan, 67
Pearlman, Laurie Anne, 102, 103
Perechodnik, Calel, 72–73
phenomenology, 89, 109
Post, Stephen, 14, 20
post-traumatic stress disorder (PTSD),
    3, 68, 82, 83, 103
Pozos, Robert, 1, 11, 12, 13, 20, 22–23

Rascher, Sigmund, 12, 13, 41
Rawls, John, 37, 38, 58
realism, 120
Reznikoff, Charles, 29–30
Rolston, Holmes, 59

Romdenh-Romluc, Komarine, 92,
    95–97
Roth, John, 73
Roth, Sol, 54, 55, 58, 60, 63
Rothberg, Michael, 104
Rousseau, Jean-Jacques, 50
Rousset, David, 67
Rubenstein, Richard, 52

Saakvitne, Karen W., 103
Sachs, Nelly, 78
Sarton, May, 51
Sartre, Jean Paul, 56
Schafer, Arthur, 23
Scott, Sarah, 95
self-blame, 76–77, 80, 83, 84
self-determination, 28, 49, 50–52,
    55–57, 61, 81
Semprun, Jorge, 74
Sen, Amartya, 57
Sherwin, Susan, 52
Singer, Peter, 33
social horizon, 98
Spiro, Howard, 22
Stauffer, Jill, 17, 18, 78
Stiffel, Frank, 29
Stone, Christopher, 33
Styron, William, 52
subjugated knowledge, 123
Sullivan, Shannon, 109
survivor guilt, 7–8
Svenson, Arne, 105–6

Taylor, Charles, 30, 67, 70
temporal objects, 89, 90, 95–97, 98,
    104, 105
testimonial injustice, 117–19
testimony, 124–26
Thomas, Laurence, 68–69, 117,
    127–28

vicarious traumatization, 102–3
Vigorito, Susan (Sara), 2, 3, 7, 15–16,
    89, 99–100
Vuilleumier, Patrik, 100

Walker, Margaret Urban, 62
Walton, Kendall, 107–8
Warburton, Nigel, 107–8
West, Paul, 94
Wiesel, Elie, 63, 72, 74
Wiesenthal, Simon, 29, 73
Wiseman, Hadas, 7

Witztum, Ely, 77
Wolff, Tobias, 36
world horizon, 105
Wylie, Alison, 121–22
Wyman, Racel, 47

Yehuda, Rachel, 69, 74, 76, 78, 82, 98–99

About the Author

Carol V. A. Quinn is professor of philosophy at Metropolitan State University of Denver and a women's studies associate. Her research interests include human rights, ethics, and feminist philosophy, and Eastern thought. She is the coauthor of *The Rashomon Tea and Sake Shop: A Philosophical Novel About the Nature and Existence of God and the Afterlife* (2016), and author of the novel, *The Glorious Life of Jessica Kraut: An Adventure in Eastern and Indigenous Religions and Philosophies* (2017).